Interpreting as a
Discourse Process

*Locating Dialect in Discourse: The Language of Honest Men
and Bonnie Lasses in Ayr*
Ronald K.S. Macaulay

English in Its Social Contexts: Essays in Historical Sociolinguistics
Edited by Tim W. Machan and Charles T. Scott

Coherence in Psychotic Discourse
Branca Telles Ribeiro

Sociolinguistic Perspectives on Register
Edited by Douglas Biber and Edward Finegan

Gender and Conversational Interaction
Edited by Deborah Tannen

Therapeutic Ways with Words
Kathleen Warden Ferrara

*Sociolinguistic Perspectives: Papers on Language in Society,
1959–1994. Charles Ferguson*
Edited by Thom Huebner

The Linguistic Individual: Self-Expression in Language and Linguistics
Barbara Johnstone

The Discourse of Classified Advertising: Exploring the Nature of Linguistic Simplicity
Paul Bruthiaux

Queerly Phrased: Language, Gender, and Sexuality
Edited by Anna Livia and Kira Hall

Claiming Power in Doctor-Patient Talk
Nancy Ainsworth-Vaughn

Kids Talk: Strategic Language Use in Later Childhood
Edited by Susan Hoyle and Carolyn Adger

Talking about Treatment: Recommendations for Breast Cancer Adjuvant Treatment
Felicia D. Roberts

Language in Time: The Rhythm and Tempo of Spoken Interaction
Peter Auer, Elizabeth Couper-Kuhlen, and Frank Müller

Interpreting as a Discourse Process
Cynthia B. Roy

Interpreting as a
Discourse Process

CYNTHIA B. ROY

New York   Oxford
OXFORD UNIVERSITY PRESS
2000

Oxford University Press

Oxford   New York
Athens   Auckland   Bangkok   Bogotá   Buenos Aires   Calcutta
Cape Town   Chennai   Dar es Salaam   Delhi   Florence   Hong Kong   Istanbul
Karachi   Kuala Lumpur   Madrid   Melbourne   Mexico City   Mumbai
Nairobi   Paris   São Paulo   Singapore   Taipei   Tokyo   Toronto   Warsaw

and associated companies in
Berlin   Ibadan

Copyright © 2000 by Cynthia B. Roy

Published by Oxford University Press, Inc.
198 Madison Avenue, New York, New York 10016

Oxford is a registered trademark of Oxford University Press

Library of Congress Cataloging-in-Publication Data
Roy, Cynthia B., 1950–
Interpreting as a discourse process / Cynthia B. Roy.
p.   cm.—(Oxford studies in sociolinguistics)
Includes bibliographical references and index
ISBN 0-19-511948-7
1. Translating and interpreting.   2. Discourse analysis.
I. Title.   II. Series
P306.2 R69   1999
418'.02—dc21   99-13649

3 5 7 9 8 6 4

Printed in the United States of America
on acid-free paper

Acknowledgments

For over twenty-five years, as I interpreted and taught interpreters, I have also talked to and studied many of them. They are too numerous to name but to them I owe a heartfelt thanks for giving me their time and attention to talk about the fascinating job they do. Two colleagues in particular—Cecilia Wadensjö and Katherine Langan—kept my interest in interpreting alive when I despaired of ever thinking about it again. They read drafts of the current text, offered suggestions, asked questions, and commented on terms, thoughts, and ideas. And they made it possible to talk about, think about, and write about interpreting and for that I am extremely grateful.

I thank Deborah Tannen for introducing me to the scholarly study of discourse analysis which I applied to the study of interpreting. I try to follow her example as a scholar, teacher, writer, and friend. Her interest, enthusiasm and support is a gift I treasure. I also thank Robert E. Johnson at Gallaudet University who encouraged and provided the means for me to pursue an inquiry into interpreting, never tired of discussing interpreting, read and edited my writing, and hired me to write and teach a master's degree in interpreting.

I thank the Student and the Interpreter who along with Deborah Tannen willingly allowed themselves to be videotaped, analyzed, and interviewed. I thank them for their faith and trust in me and for trusting that discovering interactional processes of interpreting was an important thing to do.

Other colleagues in interpreting whose friendship, interest, support and encouragement along the way have developed and sharpened my thoughts are: Robert M. Ingram, Etilvia Arjona-Tseng, Nancy Frishberg, Virginia Benmaman, Scott R. Loos, Jeffrey Davis, Elizabeth Winston, Dianne Falvo, Sharon Chasan, and many others.

During the original study I lived in Washington, D.C. while my family lived in New Orleans. Fran and Jack Hannan, Laurian and Ray

Barthe, and Craig and Karen Englert provided friendship, comfort, and sustenance for my husband and daughters. A heartfelt thanks to them all for then and now.

I also thank my colleagues in the English Department at the University of New Orleans for ten collegial years. In particular, I thank Linda L. Blanton for her support and friendship.

Anita Roberts-Long, writer, teacher, and friend, prepared the camera-ready format which took hours of learning, arranging, and adjusting the text. I am very grateful for her endless patience, persistence, and good humor. Thank you to Jordan Gilmore, a young artist, who is responsible for the art work in the text.

Most of all, I thank my husband Fred and daughters, Elizabeth and Victoria. Victoria and Elizabeth sacrificed much as their mother finished the original study and began a new job. Fred's support, interest, and encouragement through the years combined with my daughters' admiration and joy in seeing the completion of this book make for a very special occasion.

Contents

1   Prologue   3

2   Discourse   9

3   Translation and Interpretation   23

4   Turn-Taking as a Discourse Process   36

5   Analyzing Interpreted Encounters   40

6   The Meeting and the Participants   53

7   Turn Exchanges in an Interpreted   67
    Professor-Student Conference

8   Role Performance in an Interpreted   101
    Discourse Process

9   Epilogue   122

Notes   129

Bibliography   133

Index   139

Interpreting as a
Discourse Process

1

Prologue

Interpreting for people who do not speak a common language is a linguistic and social act of communication, and the interpreter's role in this process is an engaged one, directed by knowledge and understanding of the entire communicative situation, including fluency in the languages, competence in appropriate usage within each language, and in managing the cross-cultural flow of talk. Within the last decade, researchers have begun to examine the process of interpreting as embedded within a process of verbal interaction, a conversational process of people talking to each other through an interpreter, or, as I will call it here, a discourse process. Although the term *discourse* has come into wide use and is associated with a variety of disciplines, we get the first use of the term from linguistics (Harris 1952). In linguistics, discourse analysis is a familiar term generated from several branches of linguistics, often referring to analyzing "language beyond the sentence."

This book is about applying the linguistic approaches of discourse analysis to the analytical study of interpreting-about studying interpreting-as discourse, a process of conversational exchanges between two primary speakers and through an interpreter. It is also about examining how an interpreter manages the discourse process between two participants who do not speak the same language. The goals of this book are threefold: to offer a definition of interpreted events in general based on a discourse framework; to describe, analyze, and interpret the turn-taking exchanges in one interpreted event; and to discuss, from the analysis of one role performance, an interpreter's role as it is performed in interaction

3

with others. In exploring how one interpreter manages the flow of talk, one basic, crucial system was examined in detail: the turn exchange system. Exchanging turns is at the heart of the way people talk back-and-forth to each other. How turns operate and how people take speaking turns in ordinary conversational discourse has been studied frequently in linguistic approaches to discourse, and these findings are applied here.

In this study, I show that the two primary speakers take turns with the interpreter and that they participate in creating turns. The interpreter also participates in the process by creating and resolving turn phenomena, such as silence, pauses, and simultaneous talk. The interpreting event itself is influenced by both linguistic and social factors, such as the status of the participants, levels of indirectness, and explicit understanding of the progression of talk. I demonstrate that interpreters are full-scale participants in face-to-face interpreting who can influence both the direction and outcome of an interpreted event.

Examining turns during an interpreted conversation offers a relatively new empirical insight into interpreting as an interdependent, exchange process that has unique and complex features. It is a process that requires interpreter participation in organizing and managing the exchange of turns. And it requires exploring an interpreted event as a social, linguistic act governed primarily by social roles and goals during the act of communication.

Discourse and Interpreting

By the mid-1980s, linguistic studies in discourse could be found in areas such as sociolinguistics, ethnography, and conversational analysis. Although these areas differ in some of their underlying assumptions about language, about units of language as data, about ways of analyzing data, and about notions of context, they also manifest important similarities. These similarities form a central set of unifying principles for the academic study of discourse (Schiffrin 1994).

Many of these principles—such as using natural conversational data, searching and analyzing recurring patterns across speech, discovering how participants experience conversation, and exploring social and cultural factors that influence how and what people say—are some of the hallmarks of discourse analysis. Because interpreters are interpreting discourse, or conversations, they are participating in a process that has been studied and analyzed in monolingual contexts for two decades. The interpreted context can be recorded, studied, described, and analyzed in the same way to understand how an exchange of messages actually happens between two speakers of different languages.

It also means that discourse analysis is a holistic way to study human communication, a field that is expanding, absorbing, interdisciplinary, and thus utterly suited for the study of interpreting. When parts of an interpreted discourse process are isolated and when structural and functional approaches are combined, then a study can both name and describe aspects of interpreting in a way that has not occurred until recently. Such a study would also contribute to a better understanding of what components constitute interpreted events in general from what the particular description of one interpreted situation can illustrate.

A basic feature of analyzing conversations, or discourse, is that speakers take turns. Most Americans assume that in taking turns one person talks, stops, and then the next person talks. But discourse studies of conversational interaction have shown that turns do not always occur as one-at-a-time rotation and that other features, such as simultaneous talking and pauses, play a role in the back-and-forth nature of conversation. Thus, a first step is to describe how turns occur in interpreted conversations.

In any conversation, two speakers speak and they also listen. Listening is the way the next response comes about. Exchanging messages and keeping a conversation flowing allows no one to be passive. In a discourse process, the flow of talk and the contributions of all speakers must be considered to understand the meaning of any single utterance.

In addition, speakers interact to accomplish a purpose (or purposes). They bring with them different expectations about the way to accomplish their goals through talk. Moreover, they have different understandings about ways to display their intentions and to give or acquire information as well as different ways to present themselves and their perceptions about the relationships that are present.

To complicate the situation further, speakers present their ideas using different linguistic structures and also by following different automatic and unconscious conventions for using those structures. For example, inherent in language use are systems for organizing talk, such as openings and closings, turn-taking, pauses, signaling continuing thoughts, interruptions, and the presence or lack of understanding.

Recently, researchers in interpreting, many of whom are or were practitioners, have conducted studies that indicate the participation of interpreters in discourse processes (e.g., Metzger 1995; Roy 1989a; Wadensjö 1992, 1998). They have demonstrated that interpreters are involved in negotiating such things as who has the turn, asking for clarification, prompting a response or turn from a primary party, explaining what one party or another means, or explaining that one participant does not understand the other. Because the two primary speakers in interpreted events do not know the other's language,[1] the interpreter is the only participant who can logically maintain, adjust, and if necessary, repair differences in structure and use. Typically, the interpreter is the only one who knows or can easily use the conversational or discourse strategies of both languages. This means that the interpreter is an active, third participant who can influence both the direction and outcome of the event, and that event itself is intercultural and interpersonal rather than simply mechanical and technical.

The Study

The study that follows is based on the description and analysis of an interpreted meeting between a university professor and a graduate student accompanied by an interpreter. The professor speaks American English and the graduate student speaks (or uses) American Sign Language, the language of Americans who, bound together by their linguistic and cultural heritage and identified by their hearing loss, call themselves Deaf people. The use of the capital letter D signifies a cultural, ethnic meaning of the word 'deaf.' The interpreter is a young man who is fluent in American English and American Sign Language and is a working, professional, certified interpreter. They met for approximately fifteen minutes one morning before class and discussed the student's assignment. I held the camera and recorded the meeting. I also speak (or use) American English and American Sign Language and was a student in the same graduate program as the Deaf student.

One of the most important features of this study is that the analysis arises from an authentic, videotaped meeting. Typically, these three-person situations are restricted from public scrutiny due to the personal and private nature of meetings where sensitive issues might be discussed. Many of these situations are also confidential; thus, they are difficult to observe and difficult to record. The meeting analyzed in this study was open to recording by the consent of all three parties, because of their relationships to each other and the researcher, and because the meeting was not highly personal or private.

Plan of the Book

Some readers will know that the original study was done a number of years ago, in 1989 to be exact. Taking advantage of current research, I have extensively revised and updated this version so that it reflects new understandings of discourse theory and new perspectives on the role of an interpreter. Two new chapters have been written, and others differ substantially from their original versions.

Chapter 2 begins with definitions and linguistic approaches to discourse that influenced this study. Interactional sociolinguistics, conversation analysis, and ethnography of communication are the three areas that form the foundation of this study. Chapter 3 moves onto a discussion of studies in translation and interpretation that were the first to orient toward social interaction, sociolinguistics, discourse analysis, and other related disciplines. Chapter 4 then briefly scrutinizes turn-taking as it has been studied in ordinary discourse.

Chapter 5 examines the larger frame of interpreted events in general, arguing that distinctions among these events should be along interactional lines, rather than according to topic or occasion. After that discussion, I present the methods and analysis used in this case study with an explanation of interpretive studies.

In Chapter 6, the participants speak for themselves about interpreting, interpreters, languages, and the specific meeting. They were interviewed separately and provide a perspective not often solicited in academic studies of interpreting.

Chapter 7 is the analysis of turn-taking in the meeting between the professor and the student. The data revealed that although the content of the turn originates from each primary participant, the turns actually take place between each speaker and the interpreter. The interpreter participates by managing simultaneous talk, pauses and lags, and turn-taking for other turns. I show that taking turns can be both structural and functional, arising from signals within the language and also because individual speakers make decisions about the flow and nature of the talk.

In Chapter 8, I discuss the role of the interpreter. The performance of the role, especially when a primary speaker speaks directly to an interpreter, is described and analyzed in four interpreted events. More important, I consider what the interpreter's participation means for the interaction and the role of the interpreter. Chapter 9 recaps the important points of the study and suggests directions for further study.

2

Discourse

Discourse Analysis

It must seem to those slightly familiar with the term *discourse* that terms such as *sociolinguistics, discourse analysis,* and *conversation analysis* are used interchangeably. Its companion term, discourse analysis, seems to be used especially frequently, even randomly, so that it is difficult to know exactly what is meant by the term. One reason is that a number of different academic disciplines use the term to describe the methods and models they develop to understand language and human behavior. "Included are not just disciplines in which models for understanding, and methods for analyzing, discourse first developed (i.e., linguistics, anthropology, sociology, philosophy; see Van Dijk 1985), but also disciplines that have applied (and thus often extended) such models and methods to problems within their own particular academic domains, e.g., communication (Craig and Tracy 1983), social psychology (Potter and Wetherell 1987), and artifical intelligence (Reichman 1985)" (Schiffrin 1994:5).

What is meant by discourse can be a complicated and lengthy explanation. For such explanations I refer readers to Schiffrin (1994) and van Dijk (1997a, b). As van Dijk (1997a: 1) notes, discourse is a concept and a term that stands for complex phenomena and thus requires entire chapters, if not volumes, to define and describe. Within this study, however, discourse is language as it is actually uttered by people engaged in social interaction to accomplish a goal. My use of the concept is that developed in linguistics where a central goal of most discourse approaches is to discover and demonstrate how participants in a conversation make sense of what is going on (how they both create meaning and understand others' meanings) within the social and cultural context of face-to-face interaction.

In linguistics, analysts often define discourse in one of two ways: as structure or as process (van Dijk 1997a). Structural definitions focus on what constitutes a unit of discourse: "language above the sentence or above the clause" (Stubbs 1983: 1). To linguists interested in the structure of language, discourse analysis is the search for units of language that demonstrate a relationship, that occur in predictable patterns, and have rules that govern the occurrence of these elements.

In other branches of linguistics, discourse is defined as "any aspect of language use" (Fasold 1990: 65) or as a process of using language to accomplish a purpose or action. These linguists are interested in the way language functions to accomplish goals or activities in people's lives; hence, discourse is the analysis of language as it is connected to "meanings, activities, and systems outside of itself" (Schiffrin 1994: 31). Within this perspective, the structures or forms of language cannot be separated from the way people use language in their daily lives to accomplish a purpose or function (Brown and Yule 1983: 1).

Discourse as Language

Although language can be both spoken or written,[1] verbal interaction forms the basis of the analysis and interpretations in this study. Transcribing speech into written form has not been an easy task. Research by Chafe (1980, 1982) demonstrated that language is produced as units produced in chunks often defined by intonation or the completeness of a thought or idea, not as syntactically whole structures like sentences. For example, speakers often begin talking with words such as 'and' or 'but'. Speakers hesitate, repeat, stop talking, and start again—all of which cannot conform to the idea of a sentence. Often, chunks of speech are also not grammatically whole or wellformed, so to label these units as "sentences" does not suffice. Hence, as Schiffrin (1994) argues, discourse is best portrayed as "utterances," larger than other units of language, but also "the smaller unit of which discourse is comprised" (1994: 39).

Moreover, utterances are related, such as questions and answers, or they have a function, such as beginning a story. Studies that focus on how utterances are related or how utterances function are considered language use, and many studies examine how different language communities have different ways of performing similar functions (Gumperz 1982;Kochman 1981; Phillips 1974). Then utterances can include either the idea of a single utterance or the idea of a larger group of utterances that together perform a function, such as greetings or telling a story. In many studies of language, analysis often separates into an analysis of structure or an analysis of function (language use) but, as Schiffrin (1994) thoroughly demonstrates, discourse analysis can be both.

When discourse analysis focuses on structure, the task is one of identifying and analyzing utterances, discovering regularities or patterns in these utterances, and making judgments about grammatical-ness or well-formedness. When discourse analysis focuses on function, then the task is identifying and analyzing utterances as actions performed by people for certain purposes, interpreting social and cultural meanings, and justifying interpretations of the analysis. To combine these tasks is what makes discourse so vast, and to use any part of the tasks is why so many studies label themselves discourse analysis (Schiffrin 1994: 20–43).

Another reason that defining discourse as such an undertaking is that language typically includes a relationship to context. Context is tremendously broad and defined in different ways, for example, mutual knowledge, social situations, speaker-hearer identities, and cultural constructs. Within discourse analysis, context can be part of the immediate, local nature of a face-to-face interaction, as well as the larger, global nature of the social and cultural situation of a society.

Schiffrin (1994) defines discourse as "utterances," which combines and includes the distinctions above. From this perspective, utterances are structural units of language production ("language above the sentence") and functional units—a collection of inherently contextualized units of language use. This is the definition that will be used throughout the book.

Discourse as a Theoretical Construct

In *Approaches to Discourse*, Schiffrin (1994) describes and compares six linguistic approaches to discourse analysis: speech act theory, interac-tional sociolinguistics, ethnography of communication, pragmatics, con-versation analysis, and variation analysis. To describe the differences and similarities of theoretical goals and assumptions about language in each of these approaches, she analyzes and interprets actual utterances and concludes by extracting underlying principles of each approach that constitute a basis for a theory of discourse.

As Schiffrin explains, although each of these approaches originates from different, sometimes overlapping disciplines, they each attempt to answer the question, "How do we organize language into units that are larger than sentences? How do we use language to convey information about the world, ourselves, and our social relationships" (1994: viii). These questions are the questions of interpreting; we need only replace 'we' with 'an interpreter': How does an interpreter organize language into units that are larger than sentences? And How does an interpreter use language to convey information about the world, each speaker and self, and the social relationships?

Approaching interpreting as a discourse process, this study attempts to describe and analyze, first, how a discourse process, turn-taking, is organized within interpreted discourse and secondly, how participants use language to create, distribute, and maintain turns while conveying information about themselves, their relationships, and the world of interpreting encounters.

In the next sections, I present the three approaches to discourse that influenced and directed this study: interactional sociolinguistics, conversation analysis, and the ethnography of communication.

Interactional Sociolinguistics

Interactional sociolinguistics is an approach that combines anthropology, sociology and linguistics as they focus on the interplay between language, culture, and society. As a discipline, it combines description and analysis of natural data with a method for developing and adjusting interpretations of the data. This mode of analysis was developed by John Gumperz, an anthropologist, who coined the term *interactional sociolinguistics* to distinguish it from the more common type of sociolinguistics that typically examines phonological variation, and extended by Deborah Tannen, a student of Gumperz, and now an internationally known scholar. Tannen's analysis of an extended conversation, conceptualization of conversational style, and explanations of cross-cultural differences provide a model for analysis and also for humanistic interpretation.

Erving Goffman, a sociologist, is also included in this section because of his essays on the structure and organization of social interaction. His notions of the way we present ourselves to others and the way we manage interaction, or "perform our roles," affect sociolinguistic analysis (Schiffrin 1994). I discuss Goffman's work in greater detail in Chapter 8.

John Gumperz

Gumperz (1982) demonstrated that speakers in a conversation are engaged in an ongoing and immediate process of assessing others' intentions and producing responses based on the assessment of those intentions. He calls this situated or context-bound process of interpreting meaning "conversational inference" and the meanings themselves are flexible and evolve as conversations proceed (Gumperz 1977). To talk back and forth–to speak as well as listen–entails both sending and receiving multiple levels of meaning. In numerous examples, he illustrates how meanings are conveyed from multiple levels of language consisting of, but not limited to, lexical or phonological choice, syntactic patterns, use of formulaic expressions, code-switching, prosodic cues (intonation and stress), and paralinguistics (e.g., pitch, register, rhythm, and volume). Meaning is not only determined by features of language, but also, as Gumperz demonstrates, by background expectations, prior knowledge or relationships, roles, cultural knowledge, and other social knowledge.

According to Gumperz, interpreting meaning is a process of contextualization in which a listener associates certain kinds of cues within the language, called "contextualization cues," with information content on the one hand and with background expectations, or social knowledge, on the other (Gumperz 1978; 1982). Contextualization cues refer to any aspect of the surface form of utterances that, when attached to message content, function as a way of signaling how to understand what is said. These cues signal to listeners when speakers have made their points, which information is foreground and which is background, what the relationship is between comments, how what is said should be heard (whether anger or joking is meant), and many other kinds of information.

Adopting a cross-cultural perspective, Gumperz developed a method for investigating the process of contextualization cues by examining situations where they fail to work. When speakers share similar cultural backgrounds, then contextualization cues are also shared and speakers rarely misunderstand. However, when cues are not shared, misunderstandings prevail.

Schiffrin (1994) interprets his main contribution as emanating from his studies of the way people within a larger culture, who are members of smaller, distinct cultures, may share grammatical knowledge of a common language (such as English) but may also contextualize what is said differently than a member of the larger culture. In this way, messages are produced that are understood perhaps partially, but not completely, such that people take away different interpretations of what was said and done. The following is a well known example from Gumperz (1982: 30) cited by Schiffrin (1994: 7):

> Following an informal graduate seminar at a major university, a black student approached the instructor, who was about to leave the room accompanied by several other black and white students, and said:
>> (a) Could I talk to you for a minute? I'm gonna apply for a fellowship and I was wondering if I could get a recommendation?
>
> The instructor replied:
>> (b) OK. Come along to the office and tell me what you want to do.
>
> As the instructor and the rest of the group left the room, the black student said, turning his head ever so slightly to the other students:
>> (c) Ahma git me a gig! (Rough gloss: "I'm going to get myself some support.")

Before exploring how different interpretations were made by listeners, this example can serve to illustrate what interactional sociolinguistic data is and how its analysis proceeds.[2] First, a sociolinguist analyzes actual utterances that have been written down immediately or recorded on tape by an investigator. Significant to sociolinguistics is that these are not data generated from the analyst's mind or experience but rather have been actually "uttered" by a human being in a natural context. Second, examples from data are always accompanied by a brief explanation of the context—the physical setting, social roles, relationships of other participants, and other information.

Any utterance can be the focus of analysis by asking, How was this utterance understood by the people who heard it, and how did these participants arrive at their interpretation? For the sociolinguist, this entails describing the grammatical knowledge of participants and the socio-cultural knowledge that listeners rely on to understand the messages conveyed. Specifically, such an analysis accounts for the way explicit linguistic signs, such as word choice, intonation, rhythm, stress, and lexical and phonetic choices indicate speaker intent and also how social knowledge influenced a listener's interpretation. When these cues are tacitly shared by speakers, interpretive processes tend to go unremarked. However, when a listener does not react to a cue or is unaware of its function, interpretations vary, misunderstandings occur, and judgments are made.

In the preceding example, the utterance "Ahma git me a gig!" was interpreted differently by the participants in the interaction. So the question to be asked about "Ahma git me a gig!" is, what does it mean (how did the listeners arrive at their understandings), and what particular features of language and/or social situation signal that meaning?

To arrive at an understanding of what the utterance meant, interpretations are not constructed solely from the speaker's perspective but are also gathered from the participants who heard the utterance. Later, others may be asked to listen to a recording and share their understandings of the utterance(s). Then, "the analyst's task is to make an in-depth study of the selected instances of verbal interaction, observe whether or not actors understand each other, elicit participants' interpretations of what goes on, and then (a) deduce the social assumptions that speakers must have in order to act as they do, and (b) determine empirically how linguistic signs communicate in the interpretation process" (Gumperz 1982: 35).

In the analysis of the example noted here, for instance, Gumperz was able to show that most white speakers did not seem to understand the utterance other than as a lapse into dialect or saw the switch to Black English as a rejection of whites and the speaker addressing himself only to other black students. Black students, however, explained the student's remark as an attempt to justify himself by appealing to others in the group, "I'm just playing the game as we blacks must do if we are to get along in a white world," while also identifying a particular rhythm in the utterance that led them to their interpretation. Thus, features of language carry social meaning that plays a significant role in interpreting what speakers mean (see Gumperz 1982: 29–37 for a detailed explanation of this example and its interpretation).

While this example should make any interpreter wonder how they are interpreting meaning of speakers who differ in some way, such as region of the country, age, ethnicity, gender, my point here is about the analysis of natural language and how discourse analysts determine what speakers mean and how language conveys elements of meaning. Using these methods to analyze interpreted discourse is a way of understanding how the participants in an interpreted interaction understand each other at the time.

Gumperz proposed that a theory of discourse must take into account both the linguistic and sociocultural knowledge that an interlocutor must have to maintain involvement in an interaction. Accounting for such knowledge demonstrates two things: (1) meanings are jointly constructed between speakers as they talk, and (2) conversations contain internal evidence of their outcomes, that is, the ways in which participants share, partially share, or do not share, mutual conventions for meaning and how they succeed in achieving their communicative ends.

Deborah Tannen

Tannen reached a similar conclusion. She called such linguistic and social knowledge "conventions by which meaning is communicated in social interaction" (1984: 151). In *Conversational Style: Analyzing Talk Among Friends,* Tannen (1984) analyzed two and a half hours of conversation over a Thanksgiving dinner. She defined and discussed features of conversational involvement, such as topic, pacing (how relatively fast or slow one spoke), narrative strategies (in what order events are told, how speakers made their point, etc.), and expressive paralinguistics (intonation, pitch, and others), which together pattern in different ways the speech of different participants. For three of the speakers, these features combined in acceptable ways of having a conversation, but three other speakers experienced the same conversation as unusual and their participation faltered. When speakers share conventions for signaling meaning, they can be said to share a *conversational style* (Tannen 1984).

Tannen's approach to studying discourse, modeled after Gumperz, is characterized by (1) recording naturally occurring conversations; (2) identifying segments in which communication may seem to flounder or be troublesome; (3) looking for patterned differences in signaling meaning that could account for trouble; (4) playing the recording, or segment of it, back to participants to elicit their spontaneous interpretations and reactions, and also, perhaps later, eliciting their responses to the researcher's interpretations; and (5) playing segments of the interaction for other members of the cultural groups represented by the speakers to discern patterns of interpretation.

Tannen's study suggests that within an interpreted interaction speakers who do not share a common language also have conversational styles that they do not necessarily share with the interpreter. For example, Tannen (1994) has demonstrated that a discourse approach to gender and language, following in the tradition of Gumperz, can be understood by looking for differences in the way women and men signal meaning in conversation. This has great implications for interpreters: what happens when interpreters do *not* share a conversational style with one or both speakers? Many interpreters are women who interpret for men. Do they understand male strategies for asking questions or giving information? Do men understand female strategies? As her research demonstrates, "the notion of 'cross-cultural' encompasses more than just speakers of different languages or from different countries; it includes speakers from the same country of different class, region, age, and even gender" (Tannen 1985: 203).

Gumperz's analysis of brief utterances located within a social scene and Tannen's analysis of a single extended interaction via the same analytical and interpretive framework provide a rigorous methodology for analyzing conversational interactions, including interpreted conversations. Their emphasis on soliciting participant reactions and interpretations, along with close transcription of contextualization cues in language, provides a framework for going beyond a mere structural description of an interpreted encounter to an intense scrutiny of turn-taking as experienced by the participants, including phenomena such as simultaneous turn-taking.

Erving Goffman

Sociolinguists have relied heavily on the work of Erving Goffman for outlining the patterns and conditions of social interaction. Goffman (1981) proposes that two sets of conditions are required as we interact with each other. One set he calls system conditions; they center on the structural requirements of talk, for example, the ways in which people initiate talk, signal understanding, and take turns. The other set of conditions is called ritual conditions; they center on the interpersonal requirements of talk—how to manage oneself and others so as not to violate one's own demeanor or deference for another. These conditions mirror the structural versus functional perspectives of discourse discussed earlier.

Goffman focuses on social organization of the way people manifest their involvement with each other. Because this is often accomplished through language, Goffman's work heightens our understanding of the way social occasions create expectations. The process of "being involved" is a social activity "situated" in a particular time and place which includes characteristics of involvement both as a general notion (generating "norms" of conduct) and as a specific notion (generating a picture of a specific engagement, such as a teacher–student meeting). Thus, Goffman's work is particularly significant in describing the "performance" of a role, such as that of the interpreter. Language gives us specific data to digest and ponder; social interaction frameworks provide ways to unravel the expectations and/or assumptions of a role. By providing organization to contexts, Goffman illuminates the expectations and assumptions of speakers and hearers for what things mean.

Goffman is also interested in how individuals represent themselves to each other as they participate in interaction. His term *participation framework* has only recently been used in studies of interpreting (see Wadensjö 1992, 1998; Edmundson 1986). Spoken interaction organizes itself around participants' continuous assessments of self and others' roles at a turn-by-turn level. An individual's role performance depends on how all the conversational partners relate to each other. Thus, the performance of an interpreter's role, while recognizing that there are norms that are expected and/or assumed, and which may or may not differ from the actual role performance within a situated interaction, allows an analyst to describe that performance and to notice activites that may or may not fit with the prescribed role. Accordingly, we can ask about unexpected activities, such as interpreters speaking their own words.

These three scholars formed the basic framework to an interactional sociolinguistic approach to studying interpreted conversations. To form a discourse approach to turn-taking in an interpreted conversation, I turned next to the approach of conversation analysis. This approach allowed me to construct a basic, structural description of how turns worked in an interpreted interaction. For that, the seminal work on conversational exchanges by Sacks, Schegloff, and Jefferson (1974) was needed.

Conversation Analysis

According to Schiffrin, conversation analysis grows out of sociology, beginning with Harold Garfinkel who developed the approach known as ethnomethodology. Ethnomethodology was then applied specifically to conversation, most notably by Harvey Sacks, Emanuel Schegloff, and Gail Jefferson. Gumperz notes that Sacks, Schegloff, and Jefferson were "the first to systematically focus on conversation as the simplest instance of a naturally organized activity, and attempt to study the process of conversational management per se without making any a priori assumptions about the social and cultural background of the participants" (1982: 158). This work demonstrated that conversations are rule-governed and that the mechanisms which underlie speaker–listener coordination can be studied empirically. The results of these studies indicate the interactional character of conversation in the systematic ways in which conversationalists take and coordinate turns, or organize the exchange, as Sacks et al would say: "It is the systematic consequence of the turn-taking organization of conversation that it obliges its participants to display to each other, in a turn's talk, their understanding of other turns' talk" (1974: 728).

Sacks et al. were looking to create a universal model for "what might be extracted as ordered phenomena from our conversational materials which would not turn out to require reference to one or another aspect of situatedness, identities, particularities of content or context" (1974: 699).[3] Because conversation is an activity that happens among all people in various situations for various reasons, it seemed to these analysts that aspects of conversation had to be context-free and thus generalizable to all conversations. Their goal was to identify and describe the order and structure inherent in language beyond the sentence level and thus shed light on how everyday conversation is systematic and rule-governed.

Conversation analysis is a way to describe the form, or structure, of turns in a generalized way within interactional contexts. This approach provided a way of understanding the structural nature of turn-taking in interpreted events. Describing structural processes devoid of context allows for generalizations about "typical" activities. Thus conversation analysis is ideally suited for typifying what is common across interpreting, as well as what is unique in the encounter studied here.

Ethnography of Communication

"Communication" is a common concern of anthropologists and linguists. Linguists are interested with communication because communication is carried on primarily through language. Anthropologists are interested in communication because it is a part of our cultural repertoire for interacting with others and making sense of the world. Dell Hymes, an anthropologist who is considered the father of the ethnography of communication, adopted the view that culture "comprises a general 'world view': a set of assumptions and beliefs that orient and organize the way people think, feel, and act" (Schiffrin 1994: 139). He also knew that people communicate their world views primarily through language. What Hymes suggested was that "members of a culture may have available to them different forms, and be differently competent in the way they draw upon a communicative repertoire" (quoted in Schiffrin 1994: 139). And, importantly, he pointed out that although the knowledge and behaviors within a culture have to be known, available to, or used by every member, ranges of cultural behavior can be part of a culture. Thus, the ways in which we interact with each other reveals culture and also creates and negotiates culture.

Hymes proposed that scholarship focus on communicative competence: the knowledge governing appropriate and meaningful use of language, not the explicit knowledge of grammatical rules. The study of language in use—how members engage in conversation, tell stories, argue, and know how to be silent—became sociolinguistics. Ethnography of communication in anthropology becomes sociolinguistics in linguistics.

Finally, Hymes also proposed methodology for describing communicative events, a classificatory grid known as the SPEAKING mnemonic (Hymes 1972). Each letter is an abbreviation for a component of communication: scene, participants, event, key, act, instruments, genres. The SPEAKING grid is used to identify recognizable speech activities and create ways of talking about the layers of factors that affect speech activities. The largest unit is the speech situation, the social occasion in which speech may occur. The next unit is the speech event, "activities, or aspects of activities, that are directly governed by rules or norms of the use of speech" (Hymes 1972: 56). These layers continue on to the level of speech act, a verbal act that causes an action to be performed. Although this classificatory grid is not much used any more, discourse analysis still uses the terminology when discussing social encounters in which speech occurs. The main point is that discourse is a part of all these units, and all these units are part of discourse: "An ethnographic approach creates a whole that is greater than the sum of its parts: it *seeks to define* [emphasis hers] the basic notions of the other approaches to discourse simply because it views all phases and aspects of communication (from the cognitive to the political) as relative to cultural meanings" (Schiffrin 1994: 144).

Ethnography emphasizes the importance of observation and participation in speech situations and assumes that an investigator will be either a long-time observer of a communicative event or an ongoing participant in an event. To truly make sense of a social situation, an analyst has to know how the participants experience, or make sense of, the event. A participant-observer becomes familiar with the *ways of speaking* within social groups and can identify the ways in which language is tied to culturally relative views of when, how, and in what ways people should speak. Ethnography coincides with interactional sociolinguistics in describing how, for example, telling a story is different within various American ethnicities all of which speak English (Kochman 1981; Scollon and Scollon 1981).

Discourse Processes

Interpreting is the process by which people whose discourse systems are different communicate with each other in face-to-face interactions. Interpreting, then, coincides or happens within these processes and so is intimately bound up in discourse processes. Thus, interpreting inherently constructs and is constructed by many of the same elements and strategies as discourse processes, and interpreting has to be investigated while examining the discourse process. To understand how interpreting happens the analytical model of discourse analysis and the theoretical principles of discourse are used to account for the complexity and interdisciplinary nature of an interpreted event.

The analytical framework suggested by the approaches to discourse account for several themes in this study. One, the aim of this work is to *describe* the linguistic and sociolinguistic activities of one interpreter involved in an authentic interpreted event, rather than *prescribe* certain ideals or norms about interpreters or interpreting. Following Tannen (1984), the aim is to investigate an entire interaction which appears to be successful and to ask not only what the interpreter is doing but how the interpreter is managing the cross-cultural communication.

Two, discourse approaches also suggest that everyone within an interaction is a part of the interaction and thus contributing in different ways to the direction and outcome of the event. Consequently, to study the interpreter alone will not explain nor account for the "multi-directional and multi-layered processes of interpretation" (Wadensjö 1998: 8). Much of the research focuses on a one-way activity and thus focuses on the production of a text by the interpreter. When people engage in interpreted conversations, however, they see themselves as engaging in talk-oriented tasks, such as providing information, giving advice, asking questions, and so on. This poses other and different questions about the interpreter's activity and message production.

Three, an interpreter's primary concern while interpreting is to make sense of what any one person means when saying something and to convey that same sense to another person. How something is said and meant is guided by a number of relationships, the same sort of relationships that a discourse analyst uses when determining what speakers mean, such as speaker intentions, conventionalized strategies for making intentions recognizable, the meaning and function of linguistic forms, the sequential context of utterances, discourse genre, the social context, and a cultural framework of beliefs and actions (Schiffrin 1994). These relationships are the foundation of the complex process of discourse and interpreting. Thus, in a manner of speaking, interpreters are discourse analysts, and the speech event of interpreting is a discourse process.

3

Translation and Interpretation

Translation

Eugene Nida has suggested that the "significance of translation as an act of communication has been overlooked or underestimated" and has called for translation to be studied as a communicative event (1964: xx). With the publication of Brislin's (1976) edited collection *Translation*, many authors began to call for studying translation (which is text-centered) and its related field, interpreting (which is speech-centered), as communicative processes. In the introduction, Brislin notes: "There is a recent study area in the social and behavioral sciences that is devoted to just these aspects of communication in social settings. It is called sociolinguistics, and it has been described in a number of places (Ervin-Tripp 1969; Gumperz and Hymes 1972)" (1976: 77).

Nida's point was that sociolinguistic theory focuses on language performance which, in turn, focuses the translator's attention on the person who receives the message. "Because translating always involves communication within the context of interpersonal relations, the model for such activity must be a communication model, and the principles must be primarily sociolinguistic"(1976: 78). Nida advocated sociolinguistic theory because he knew that translation processes needed to account for a myriad of factors—interpersonal relations, extralinguistic features, and linguistic, cultural, and social variants—that influence the way a message is formed and understood. As Nida called for this change, sociolinguistics had just begun to account for these same social factors as they influenced meaning when language was used within a particular social event or institution. What Gumperz and Hymes made clear in the preface to *Directions in Sociolinguistics: The Ethnography of Commu-*

nication (1972) is that the primary theoretical goal of sociolinguistic investigation is the concept of *communicative competence*: what a speaker needs to know to communicate effectively in culturally significant settings. Communicative competence includes not only the grammatical competence a speaker has but the knowledge of culturally appropriate "ways of speaking," such as how to ask for information, give praise, complain, joke, and so on. This had an impact on translation because translations are written to specific audiences for specific reasons and to accomplish specific goals. Translators had to know how societies or cultures used words, phrases, and sentences in order to interpret them to an audience in a meaningful way. Thus, translation began to focus on how the listener or listeners would understand a message and how insufficient it was to expect a form-to-form translation.

In Brislin (1976), Anderson, a sociologist, speculated on the role of translators (he included interpreters in this usage) in *social* situations, and believed that, as such, these situations could be analyzed as socially constructed situations with underlying rules and conditions and accordingly, an analysis would reveal all the ways in which interpreters were functioning in such situations. His speculation was that the interpreter "is likely to exert considerable influence on the evolution of group structure and on the outcome of the interaction" (Anderson 1976: 209). He also commented that understanding the role of interpreters should enlighten our understanding of interaction between people whose different statuses and backgrounds differ.

Anderson's main contribution lies in his outline of a typical interpreting event: a situation that is social in nature and constituted primarily of three people—two primary participants and an interpreter. One primary participant is typically a representative of government authority, such as a police officer, a officer of the court, or a representative of social services, such as a doctor, caseworker, or other and who typically speaks the majority or prestige language. A second primary participant is typically a person in need of services and who typically speaks a minority or less prestigious language. The third participant is the interpreter. Each of these representatives has a particular role, and Anderson emphasized that by definition, interpreters are bilingual, and most likely, the only bilingual in the situation. "The two monolingual actors would be unable to communicate with each other without his aid—except through a primitive set of gestures" (1976: 210).

In a later article, Anderson (1978) also noted in a number of interviews with spoken language interpreters that most agreed that only a small percentage of their work was conference interpreting (a term for interpreting a single speaker to a largely nonresponsive audience). His analysis is one of the first to point the way toward a discourse framework by pointing out the significance of participant roles and elements for interpreted events.

More recently, Shuy (1987, 1990) has stressed the need for research into translation and interpreting as a communicative event suggesting that sociolinguistics and its subfield discourse analysis are fields uniquely designed to study interpreting and interactive events.

Cognitive Approaches to the Interpreting Process

Initially, research on interpreting processes was done by cognitive psychologists and psycholinguists interested in the simultaneous processing task of listening, interpreting, and speaking. While much of the research had been experimental, some of the more recent research has used conference interpreters as they worked, all of which has focused on interpreter error in order to locate cognitive breakdowns which highlight information processing stages (Cokely 1984; Gerver 1974; Lambert 1983; Moser-Mercer 1978).

Gerver (1976) summarized the research he surveyed by suggesting that a model based on theories about human information processing, with particular attention to memory and attention, be adapted to represent the cognitive processes involved in simultaneous interpreting. Then he outlined a model with two caveats: one, that the flow chart of human information processing "refers only briefly to the processes involved in decoding the source language message and its subsequent encoding in the target language," and the other, that the model is essentially psychological rather than a linguistic description of simultaneous interpretation" (1976: 196).

He concluded with a warning that this kind of model is only a first approximation and that further analysis of situational, personal, and linguistic factors is needed. As he clearly indicates in his summary, "Professional interpreters might, for instance, object that failing to take into account such nonverbal factors as the presence or absence of the actual source language speaker, or an audience diminishes the value of conclusions based on experimental findings" (1976: 202).

Moser-Mercer (1978) elaborated on Gerver's model by further expanding the stages of cognitive activities involved in understanding and producing language. Both of these models attempt to define the interpreter's organization and access of syntactic and semantic information.

Moving away from translation theories based on contrastive linguistics, Seleskovitch, a teacher of conference interpreters in France, also moved toward psycholinguistics for explanations of how interpreters should not be focusing on word-level equivalents but rather on the *sense* that a text conveys. She wrote, "The sensing of what is meant as opposed to knowing a language as such is the very foundation of interpretation"(1977: 28). She argued that interpreters should render the sense of a message or idea through a three-step process of understanding, visualizing, and re-creating the message in the target language.

Cokely (1984) argued that these models are information processing models that view the interpreting process as concerned primarily with language transfer, which does not account for the fact that "the interpreter mediates between two individuals and communities as well as mediating between two languages" (1984: 10). Cokely's model, a psycholinguistic model of the cognitive stages of processing, was produced from analyzing the miscues (errors) of six interpreters who interpreted for speakers giving lectures at a conference. Cokely produced a taxonomy of the major cognitive stages of an interpreting process: message reception, preliminary processing, short term message retention, semantic intent realization, semantic equivalence determination, syntactic message formulation, and message production.

The first communicative model of simultaneous interpreting was developed by Ingram (1974). In this early model, the interpreter is represented as a channel in a communication-binding context with a source and a receiver. Ingram (1985) revised his earlier model to include the multicode, multichannel nature of interpreting as a complex semiotic process. In this model, the interpreter must decode, transfer, and recode "a multiplicity of messages in a multiplicity of interwoven codes with every single act of interpretation" (1985: 111). Ingram's work pointed the way toward the notion of multiple ways in which meaning is communicated and the need to uncover such complex possibilities.

Sociolinguistic and Discourse Studies in Translation and Interpretion

In 1990 two books arrived on the international scene and began to change the course of research and theory in translation and interpreting: one, a discourse approach to translation and the other a sociolinguistic approach to interpreting. These two studies and, as many of the studies that follow note, come to similar conclusions: (1) The interpreter is doing more than transferring the linguistic content of messages; (2) It is necessary to study the interaction among all participants; (3) To study interpreting effectively requires recording and transcribing talk; (4) Meanings can be understood only when considered in the light of the relationship of the participants, their intentions, their goals, discourse sequences, and other elements of discourse; and (5) Interpreters are negotiating the way messages are understood by others, not just the meaning of words.

Basil Hatim and Ian Mason

Hatim and Mason (1990) begin *Discourse and the Translator* by commenting on all the ways scholars have differentiated the process of translating, including language functions, genre versus literature, or functions of the text. What they conclude is that these differentiations confuse, widen, and obfuscate the discussion without attending to the similarities, a focus which would allow building a common theoretical base. What they propose is to consider all texts as evidence of a "communicative transaction taking place within a social framework," which changes translating from restrictions formed for a particular field, such as religious, literary, or scientific, to that "which can include such diverse activities as film subtitling and dubbing, simultaneous interpreting, cartoon translating, abstracting and summarizing, etc." (2). Their central concern is to show "translating as a communicative process which takes place within a social context" and to provide a model for translation that will allow for greater consistency and a common vocabulary for discussing translation issues (3).

Traditionally, books of translation tend to review and critique a translated product or offer principles for doing translation. Hatim and Mason suggest a perspective of translation as a process which involves readers in negotiating textual meaning produced by a translator. They view a translated text as evidence of a transaction, a way of exploring, describing, and analyzing a translator's decision making process.

In their discussion of trends in linguistics and translation, they note that "these developments (context-sensitive linguistics, sociolinguistics, discourse studies, and artificial intelligence) have provided a new direction for translation studies. It is one which restores to the translator the central role in a process of cross-cultural communication and ceases to regard equivalence merely as a matter of entities within texts" (35). This quote echoes Anderson's earlier point that the interpreter's role is crucial in the process, and once again recommends that sociolinguistics and discourse studies are the best ways to study such a role.

Hatim and Mason begin to explore sociolinguistic and discourse notions, such as register (a sociolinguistic term), and to discuss its usefulness for studying context, noting that the term has become increasingly hard to define, and thus, useless. As they move toward a discussion of conversation analysis (noting exactly the questions that motivate this study), they state:

> For the time being, however, the preoccupations of conversation analysis—and therefore its research findings so far— have to do with issues such as turn-taking in conversation, adjacency pairs (question/answer, greeting/greeting, etc.), preferred responses (the rank order of expectedness among possible second parts of adjacency pairs), and so on. As such, they are more obvious relevance to the process of liaison interpreting than to written translating. How do interpreters cope with the management of turn-taking?

> Is there always a need for interpreters to intervene? To what extent and how can they intervene successfully? These are the kinds of question to which empirical research in interpreting studies should address itself. Yet unfortunately, no substantial empirical work has been carried out into these phenomena, partly due to the inaccessibility of recorded data. Nevertheless, the scope for research here is tremendous. (81)

In this lengthy discussion, they argue eloquently for (a) empirical, or data-driven, research in interpreting, and (b) the focus of analysis to be discourse phenomena of the type which occurs in studies of monolingual conversations. Their pointed questions about the role of the interpreter can be answered only by studying recorded data via sociolinguistic and discourse methods. This study answers that call.

Susan Berk-Seligson

That same year, Berk-Seligson's (1990) ground-breaking study of hundreds of hours of courtroom interpreting also appeared. Her major finding was that interpreters became actively involved participants in the discourse process of courtroom proceedings. She found that court interpreters are "intrusive elements in court proceedings far from being the unobtrusive figure whom attorneys and judges would like her to be" (96).

For example, ordinary court procedures, as well as other participants, shift attention to interpreters on a regular basis in a courtroom. Judges have to introduce and swear in interpreters, thus calling attention to them as another participant in a judicial process, as well as calling attention to the notion of accuracy in translation. In the voir dire process with jurors, attorneys ask directly if the presence of an interpreter is bothersome. More important, what will show up repeatedly in future studies is that attorneys and judges often resort to addressing the interpreter rather than the witness when they ask their questions.

Berk-Seligson also demonstrated that interpreters were not always "just" interpreting. They ask for permission to speak when proceedings become confusing; they ask for clarification of a term or idea; they halt proceedings when they hear a word they do not understand; they ask for repetition of what they did not hear. At times, they report difficulty, such as clarifying ambiguity, dialect differences, or grammatical problems. Finally, witnesses, defendants, plaintiffs, and other participants within the court make side comments to interpreters or talk to them directly. Moreover, she provided examples of interpreters who controlled the flow of testimony by urging or prompting a witness to speak or by getting witnesses and defendants to be silent (86). For example, interpreters say to witnesses "do you understand?" or "answer!" or "answer, please." Interpreters also ask questions of witnesses such as "what?" or "I didn't hear you."

Berk-Seligson's study is the first sociolinguistic study of interpreters to follow traditional sociolinguistic studies by recording hundreds of hours of data, looking for patterns and variations in the speech of the participants (see Labov 1972). More important, it is the first published study to observe, describe, and evaluate interpreters' active participation in the role of one who passes on what others say and in the role as an individual participant in a speech situation.

Cecilia Wadensjö

Wadensjö's (1998) book, *Interpreting as Interaction*, is about "interpreter-mediated conversations as a mode of communication, about interpreters and their responsibilities, about what they do, what they think they should do and what others expect them to do in face-to-face, institutional encounters" (2). The heart of her book examines empirical data–recorded, interpreter-mediated encounters within medical, legal, and social services settings–to show us what interpreters and primary speakers actually do as they come together and what they think they are doing when they talk to each other.

Wadensjö's work (1992, 1998) is theoretically grounded in analytical frameworks of the nature of social organization (Goffman) and in the dialogic theory of language and interaction (Bakhtin). She offers a seminal perspective of the interpreter as an engaged actor solving not only problems of translation but problems of mutual understanding in situated interaction. Applying a dialogic framework revealed that interpreting consists of two interdependent activities–translation and coordination–established by the fact that interpreters create two kinds of talk: talk that is generated from relaying a message, and talk that is generated from the interpreter to assist (or mediate) the flow of talk. "When the interpreter's role performance is investigated as *interaction* [italics hers], however, when the interpreter is studied in relation to a relevant audience or *role others* (Goffman), it becomes self-evident that the dialogue interpreter must be conceived of as both *relayer* and *co-ordinator* (1992: 266).

She also provides examples of utterances directed *at* the interpreter and *from* the interpreter which are not about the content of the relayed message. Thus, the progression of talk is both a co-ordinated activity among the participants, and a responsibility of the interpreter. "In an interpreter-mediated conversation, the progression and substance of talk, the distribution of responsibility for this among co-interlocutors, and what, as a result of interaction, becomes mutual and shared understanding–all will to some extent depend on the interpreter's words and deeds" (195).

Elaborating further on interpreter rights and responsibilities, Wadensjö problematizes 'understanding' in conversation and its opposite 'miscommunication' by showing three different ways interpreters handle miscommunication events while on duty. The ways in which interpreters deal with miscommunication reveals their perspectives on what constitutes sufficient understanding among the participants.

In her discussion of "replaying by displaying" and "replaying as re-presenting," Wadensjö explores how interpreters relate as narrators of others' speech to convey impressions of self as a person using others' words or to "re-present the expressiveness of preceding talk" (247). Through language, interpreters can distance themselves from an utterance they speak, a distinction that results in the primary participants' better understanding of the message. Her point is that even when interpreters move further away from the role of strictly transferring, it *benefits* the goal-oriented exchange. By noticing this distancing, it demonstrates how the reality of interpreting does not reflect the idealized pedagogy about how interpreters do their work. Notably, in manifesting this distance, we get an idea of personal style.

While the old adage to "just translate and translate everything" is a useful shorthand for explaining interpreting to lay persons and newcomers, it is not useful for explanations needed to define interpreting as a profession and to define the actual rights and responsibilities that define the everyday experience of interpreting work. Wadensjö has opened a vast new perspective for understanding, researching and teaching the work of interpreters.

Wadensjö offers, in a seminal way, the perspective of interpreter as engaged actor solving not only problems of translation but problems of mutual understanding. Hers is the first full-length work to suggest that we can understand the task of interpreting much better if we look to a perspective which accounts for the interactivity of the primary participants, rather than looking only at the interpreter and the interpreted message. The frameworks of social interaction and dialogic linguistics provide, again for the first time, a deeply theoretical understanding of the complex nature of participating in an interpreter-mediated encounter. Wadensjö differs from Berk-Seligson in attempting to understand interpreters as they do their job, not evaluating them against idealized and unsubstantiated notions of "ideal" practice.

When Goffman (1981) introduced his notions of participation framework, the complex ways in which speakers participate in a conversation, he did not explore the complexities that exist within the role of listener. Wadensjö does this. She develops the notion of reception formats corresponding to that of 'production formats.' Distinguishing between production roles is a way of making explicit in what sense speakers display their own or others' opinions or attitudes; the gain in distinguishing different modes of listening is to more thoroughly elucidate how individuals demonstrate "their own opinions and attitudes concerning rights and responsibilities in interaction" (92).

An interpreter's role, as both a social role and a role that performs an activity, is realized through interaction with others. With analytical precision and detail, she explains how interpreters both listen and speak within shifting stances of their own participation, shifting from relaying to coordinating the interaction. Thus, they change the level and degree of their participation. Wadensjö's work is significant because it profoundly changes the current vision, or ideology, of what interpreters are doing. In fact, the *"pas de troix"* (Wadensjö's expression) is the basic, fundamental event of interpreting and other models should be seen as deriving from it. It changes teaching the process of interpreting and certification practices for interpreters.

Critical Link: Conference on Community Interpreting

Since Wadensjö, more and more researchers are turning toward an interactive, discourse-oriented approach to interpreting. In 1995, *Critical Link*, an international conference on community interpreting, took place in Canada. *Community interpreting* has come to be the term for face-to-face, interactive interpreting in legal, health, social service, and other community-oriented settings. The edited collection of the proceedings is a proliferation of papers affirming the new perspective of a discourse approach to interpreting and the active role of the interpreter. Researchers around the world, many of whom are also interpreters, are defining, examining, analyzing interpreted interaction, and reporting similar results.

Fenton (1997) of New Zealand reports on the way interpreters influence proceedings in courtrooms, noting as did Berk-Seligson that interpreters are visible verbal participants. In studies on courtrooms in New Zealand, Fenton finds: "Interpreters in the courtroom are far from being perceived by everyone else in the courtroom as non-thinking, mechanical or electronic devices, but rather as men and women in possession of special skills, the application of which requires good judgement and integrity, and who can be held accountable for their performances" (33). Dimitrova (1997) of Sweden, analyzing the interpreted interaction between doctors speaking Swedish and patients speaking Spanish, noticed simultaneous talking, interruptions, and turn-taking by interpreters and the primary interlocutors. In her discussion, she notes that interpreters are at the center of the turn-taking process and therefore training programs should teach students how to interrupt primary speakers in order to avoid simultaneous talk and to claim speaking turns. Fowler (1997) of England suggests that although the law would like to see the interpreter as a conduit, it is clear that when breakdowns occur, magistrates want the interpreters to "fix it": "The magistrates I interviewed did not blame the interpreter for communication breakdown, but they certainly made it clear that when breakdowns occurred it was the responsibility of the interpreter to rectify them" (197). Each of these researchers is using sociolinguistic research and discourse analysis to describe and analyze the role of interpreters.

Melanie Metzger

In 1995, Melanie Metzger concluded her sociolinguistic study of a professional interpreter in a pediatric examination and of student interpreters role-playing a medical interview between a doctor and a deaf person. Using a sociolinguistic approach, including Goffman's participant framework, her analysis revealed that eight percent of the professional interpreter's total talk, or 29 utterances, was not that of relaying the talk of either of the primary participants. Of the 29 utterances, most were directed to the deaf patient, and only one to the doctor, one to the nurse, and two to the researcher and videographer, who was Metzger herself.

Much of the professional interpreter's talk arose from the assumptions and expectations of the participants which came to light during the interaction. "That is, some information is available within the interaction and originates among the interlocutors, but for some reason the interpreter must generate an utterance in order to fulfill the goal of relaying that information" (151). These "relays" came about from discourse confusion such that the interpreter had to identify the original speaker of the utterances, repeat talk because of the overlapping talk, or ask for clarification because of distractions or lack of background knowledge.

Like Berk-Seligson and Wadensjö, Metzger's analysis revealed the interpreter generating utterances to manage conversational flow. Many of these utterances were attention-getting strategies, for example, to get the attention of the deaf participant who begins to talk when the doctor is not finished talking. "Both the existence and variety of these utterances and of the footings they represent indicate that the interpreter does influence interpreted interactive discourse" (1995: 205). She notes that although interpreters function as participants, they are also "far more constrained in their participation than other participants" (248). All in all, a large portion of interpreter utterances are retellings or reports of what other participants have said.

Using a structural form, *adjacency pairs,* identified by conversation analysts, Metzger proposes that an interpreted event is the interaction between overlapping dyadic talk. That is, one speaker talks to the interpreter and although the interpreter then transfers the message to the next primary speaker, both speakers are talking to, responding to, and taking turns with the interpreter. In the example, Metzger uses greetings, one form of adjacency pair, to describe the unique form of embedding within interpreted conversations. In this example, G refers to the greeting, such that G1 is the first part of an adjacency pair, and G2 is the second part of the greeting pair:

G1	Participant:	Hello (Language A)
G1a:	Interpreter:	Hello (Language B)
G2a:	Participant:	Hello (Language B)
G2	Interpreter:	Hi (Language A)

In this exchange, participant 1 offers a greeting; the interpreter translates the greeting to the other participant who responds by saying hello and the interpreter then passes on the greeting back to the first participant. Language pair part B is embedded within the language A exchange. The interpreter exchanges greetings with participants in their own languages; thus, the interaction, Metzger argues, is organized at one level as a dyad between the two participants who speak the same language.

From the professional interpreter's actions and utterances, Metzger's analysis revealed the ways in which the interpreter was avoiding or minimizing her influence in the interpreted interaction. Some strategies, such as providing minimal responses to direct questions, allow for primary participant expectations of discourse with a third participant, while keeping that participation minimal to return to the focus of the meeting. Once again, Metzger, like Berk-Seligson, Wadensjö and others, has demonstrated that interpreters are participants in a discourse process, influencing the course and direction of an interaction. Like Wadensjö, Metzger has shown that interpreters shift their stance from strictly relaying to a more overt participatory status to assist in communication and back to relaying, and that they influence interaction via their own participation. The paradox of neutrality is, as Metzger puts it, the question whether interpreters should pursue more coordinating activity or attempt to minimize wherever and whenever possible.

These studies and the one herein point the way toward an extraordinary change in perspective in translation and interpreting. Accepting this new direction will mean changes in practice, teaching and testing. Most of all, as Hatim and Mason noted, it restores to the translator and interpreter a central role in the process of cross-cultural communication which takes note of their expertise and celebrates it.

4

Turn-Taking as a Discourse Process

Turn-Taking

Turn-taking is a basic, specific discourse property that can be observed, described, analyzed, and explicated. Examining turns during an interpreted conversation offers a still new, relatively unexplored, empirical insight into interpreting as a discourse process. Turn-taking in interpreting has unique and complex features that actively involve the interpreter in organizing, managing, constraining, and directing the flow of talk. Interpreters make decisions to manage and orchestrate turns due to and because of the surface linguistic meanings and the social meanings inherent in the situation and its expectations. Moreover, all the participants are taking turns based on both signals within the language and based on their own sense of rights and obligations when talking.

The Sacks, Schegloff, and Jefferson Model

Any observer of face-to-face interaction can see that talk proceeds through a sequence of turns. The Sacks, Schegloff, and Jefferson (1974) study posits this observation as one of the basic tenets of conversation. Although it appears effortless, turn-taking is a system that organizes speaker change and its recurrence. The Sacks, Schegloff, and Jefferson model has been applied to many languages; thus an application of the Sacks et al. model to interpreting, talking across languages, might uncover a similar, generalized system and rules. The turn-taking model is also applicable because it is regulated by the requirements of how speakers organize sequences of talk in face-to-face interaction, not by a particular grammar or by meanings.

Consequently, the turn-taking model *typically* deals with single transitions, or turns, at a time, while allocating the "next turn." Although the system deals with one turn at a time serially, it also deals with all the possible ways turns can occur. Turn-taking, then, demonstrates the "thoroughly interactional character of conversation" (1974: 728).

In specifying how turns are exchanged, the system also describes and accounts for many apparent facts about conversation. The rules provide for a description of silence between turns and between speaking times. They also allow transforming one type of silence into another kind of silence. For example, a gap (a between-turn silence) can be transformed into a pause (an in-turn silence) if the silence is ended by further talk by the same speaker (Sacks et al. 1974: 715, n 16). The system accounts for speaker change and its recurrence, yet does not make it an automatic occurrence. Briefly, the model specifies several things about turns: (1) generally one participant talks at a time; (2) overlap is common, but brief; (3) transitions with gap and overlap happen although transitions with no gap and overlap are common; (4) turn order varies; (5) turn length varies; and (6) the distribution of turns is not specified in advance. The Sacks et al. model provides a basic system of accounting for turns, as well as withstanding the test of time. Although other factors account for the why of turns, this model provided a categorization for turns described in the analysis.

A Discourse Approach to Turns

Researchers (Bennett 1981; Edelsky 1981; Murray 1985; Tannen 1984, 1989b) who came after Sacks et al. have pointed out that some of the "rules" postulated in the model are not necessarily the way conversation "typically" works. They argue that there can be more than one speaker at a time and also that speakers begin talking for reasons other than recognition of a turn possibility. Tannen (1989b) has demonstrated repeatedly that many ethnicities in America do not interpret "speaking at the same time" as one speaker interrupting another speaker.

Bennett (1981) argues that defining simultaneous talk by describing its form or structure leads to false conclusions because such talk can be understood in contradictory ways in different discourses. Overlap, he claims, describes the actual occurrence of two people talking at the same time whereas interruption is an interpretation that conversational participants use to make decisions (and judgments) about rights and obligations within a situation.

Tannen (1984), in analyzing a Thanksgiving dinner among friends, found that overlapping speech was both comfortable and well received when used by participants of similar conversational styles. These participants describe overlapping talk as showing interest and involvement. Tannen (1989b) also argues that overlapping speech is often neither intended nor perceived as interruption and that perceived interruptions are often not the fault or intention of a speaker but rather the result of style differences, the interaction of two differing turn-taking systems.

The point is that people make determinations about their conversational exchanges, including when to take a turn, based on factors other than syntactic units. Turns come about as speakers understand the purpose of talking together, their roles and relationships, and how a speech event is emerging in particular and in its relationship to the larger world.

O'Connell et al. (1990) review turn taking studies based on the Sacks et al. model and agree with sociolinguistic and discourse studies that the Sacks et al. model cannot stand alone, given studies that demonstrate *"continuous* participation on the part of all the interlocutors" (365). As discourse analysts argue, turn-taking is not a conversational mechanism operating outside of speaker intent, but rather depends on conversational purposes. They call for context-sensitive approaches for redefining turns, back-channeling, overlap, and interruption that would remain consistent across research projects. This study answers this call to merge the Sacks et al. model with a context-sensitive analysis of interpreted discourse.

Summary

Turn-taking then is a discourse process which can help us understand how the exchange of messages actually takes place. Turn-taking is also a feature of discourse that allows for both a structural and functional analysis. In the chapters that follow, I have four goals: (1) to begin outlining the universal elements of an interpreted event; (2) to describe the turn-taking elements and process of an interpreted event as a discourse system; (3) to illuminate how this particular event is a process of each participant engaging with others; and (4) how the role of the interpreter is a result of making decisions that are communicative in nature. The Sacks et al. model helps descriptively because it organizes turn taking sequences as they operate within interpreting. Discourse analysis shows how turns come about through the deliberate, intentional purposes of all three participants. Both of these approaches help an analyst organize and interpret data.

5

Analyzing Interpreted Encounters

Describing Interpreting

Interpreting has only recently been analyzed in the discourse events where it most frequently occurs, that is, settings which are small, generally private in nature, and in which three or more people come together to accomplish a purpose, a task or a goal while they talk (Roy 1989a; Wadensjö 1992, 1998; Metzger 1995, 1999). Although there is a call worldwide for interpreters to sort out and label the varieties of this setting (Roberts 1995), taxonomies or categories cannot be helpful until we sort out what interpreted events have in common and what features of those events make them separate. Or, until we decide, as Gentile (1995) suggests, "that what we are talking about is simply *interpreting*" no matter how many people, what type of discourse situation, or what speed of translation is involved (118). Currently, theorists, analysts, practitioners, and others observe and describe interpreting through their own lenses, be they disciplinary or personal. However, interpreting is a discipline that is and must be connected primarily to language; it will be through the lens of language study that primary elements are most readily identified. Through the lens of language as discourse, aided by models of the interaction of language and social life (Hymes 1972), the multiple relationships between linguistic means and social meaning are brought to light. Hymes suggested that constructing models of this interaction is an empirical problem which calls for description that is both ethnographic and linguistic. To develop models, Hymes warns, there must be adequate descriptions of interaction, and such "descriptions call for an approach that partly links, but partly cuts across, partly builds between the ordinary practices of the disciplines" (41). Although Hymes is referring to linguistics, anthropology, and other social sciences, we can extrapolate the warning that there must be adequate descriptions of interpreting and approaches that link, cut across, and build upon other disciplines.

This chapter attempts to describe and define some of the basic elements that constitute an interpreted event in ways that begin to meet Hymes's call. The second part of the chapter explains the procedures used to analyze the interpreted event that is the focus of this study.

A Speech Event Called Interpreting

The terminology Hymes used to describe social scenes where language is central is still current (e.g.Schiffrin 1994); thus, I will also use this terminology to refer to and name interpreted events. Because the linguistics means must combine with the social framework, Hymes begins with the now customary expression (to anthropologists, ethnographers, and sociolinguists) *speech community*, which he defines as "a community sharing rules for the conduct and interpretation of speech, and rules for the interpretation of a least one linguistic variety" (1972: 54). Each primary participant in an interpreted meeting is a member of one or more speech communities, and interpreters must be members of at least the two speech communities represented by the primary participants, recognizing that not every aspect of a community's cultural assumptions and beliefs are necessarily shared by each member.

Within speech communities are communicative "units" that are "in some recognizable way bounded or integral" (1972: 56). The largest such unit is the *speech situation*: the social occasion in which speech may occur (e.g., meals, parties, etc.). Although speech situations provide a setting where speech might, or might not occur, they are also social occasions where more than speech might take place. The next unit is *speech event*: "activities or aspects of activities, that are directly governed by rules or norms of speech" (1972: 56). Although there is still a smaller unit, a *speech act*, the speech event unit is important in defining the units of interpreted speech events. Speech events are also discourse events, and many of our "typical" discourse events are also interpreted.

Broadly speaking, interpretation shares most of the characteristics of ordinary discourse situations and events with one extraordinary exception: the two primary speakers do not have a common language.

Any meeting between these two speakers, however, can be conducted only according to one speech community's rules and norms. It is generally true that speakers of a minority language typically go to speakers of a majority language for some kind of service, thus, it is this speech community's norms that are typically followed. For example, in the United States, Spanish-speaking patients go to see American English-speaking doctors and become participants in the speech event of a medical exam which is conducted according to standard American cultural "ways of speaking" in a medical exam.

For many non-English-speaking people, it is possible that medical practices and services are not conducted in the same manner and with the same expectations as American exams. So even with experience, new expectations could come to light during ongoing visits. Typically, discourse events of the majority culture are only slightly familiar to speakers of a minority language or, even if familiar, are still a mystery in terms of acting "appropriately." The point here is that, typically, an interpreter and two speakers are participating in a speech or discourse event of one speech community such that one participant does not speak the majority language and also may not know how to contend with variation in the event.

In any one society the range of speech situations is extensive and the range of speech events within them is also extensive. Categorizing these events meaningfully for practitioners, researchers, and students has been less than adequate. Traditionally, interpreted events have been characterized in a number of ways: (1) by institutional settings, such as educational, medical or legal where interpreting takes place; (2) by the language group with which an interpreter is associated (Spanish, ASL, Russian, etc.); (3) by the mode of interpreting (simultaneous, consecutive, translation, etc.); (4) by the number or type of participants (conference, community, liaison, ad hoc, one-on-one, etc.); or (5) by the social occasion (wedding, graduation, retirement, etc.).

Descriptions based on the number of speakers and the extent of their participation use terms like *conference interpreting* and *platform interpreting* to mean one person speaking for an extended length, such as giving a speech, and an audience which is largely nonresponsive. *Community interpreting* or *one-on-one interpreting* is typically taken to mean two primary speakers (although others may be present) with an interpreter and is "done to assist those immigrants who are not native speakers of the language to gain full and equal access to statutory services (legal, health, education, local government, social services)" (Collard-Abbas 1989: 81). There is also *liaison interpreting* or *small group interpreting* which means that the number of primary speakers is more than two, all of whom are participating in some way, such as a therapy group or a committee meeting.

In some interpreting papers and texts, descriptions refer to details of the surface form of the message, such as Sign Language interpreting, where terms include *sign to voice* and *voice to sign*, or *voicing*. In spoken language interpreting, it simply refers to the names of the languages involved, that is Swedish to Russian, or Spanish interpreting, and so on.

Everyone recognizes the abundance of labels for interpreting. At the first international conference on *community interpreting*, there were calls for defining and refining the practice of community interpreting and its related subspecialities, such as legal interpreting (Benmaman 1995). Both Gentile (1995) and Roberts (1995) point to the numerous designations of what community interpreting includes. This labeling variety is cumbersome, unwieldy, and remarkable only for the settings that are left out. Attempts to clarify this run into problems as labelers peer through their own lenses to identify aspects of the interpreting event.

Using any of the above criteria makes it difficult to select elements that are the same, or those that are different, or to construct a taxonomy, or categorization, of interpreted discourse events. For example, what kind of interpreting is a lecture about ethics to medical students at a university called? Is it an educational setting? a medical setting? a conference or platform setting? a philosophical setting? Clearly these choices are confusing, overlapping, and not helpful.

I would suggest, instead, that divisions be made along an interactional dimension. An interpreted event in which conversation is occurring, in which participants take turns, change topics and in which information is only part of the goal, is a notably different interaction from an event in which there is a single speaker, in which turn-taking is minimal or nonexistent and in which the focus is on the message content, or information.

Conversational interaction typically occurs in a group composed of a small number of people, in which interaction is characterized by taking turns, utterance pairs, such as questions and answers, responses, changing topics and other discourse features. Within these conversational events, participants come together to accomplish specific goals while they present and negotiate meanings and relationships through the exchange of talk. Because these exchanges are layered with linguistic, social, and cultural meanings, interpreters are required to be more active in the discourse process themselves in order to manage communication (Roy 1989a; Wadensjö 1992; Metzger 1995).

Interaction is restrained in situations in which one speaker delivers a content-oriented talk to an audience that is expected, in general, not to respond. In these discourse events, the face-to-face interaction between participants is reduced and the attention is focused on the content of the speaker's talk. These distinctions are important for interpreters. Interpreters instinctively mold their behavior and the nature of their participation around these dimensions of interaction between and among participants.

Defining Interpreted Events

Single Speaker Interpreted Events

In discourse events where a single participant talks, the speaker chooses the topic(s), decides when to begin, when to end (although there may be a specified time limit), does most of the speaking, and decides whose and what questions, if any, will be answered. The audience is typically limited in its responses. Generally, audiences are not expected to engage actively in talk with the speaker other than to provide occasional verbal or nonverbal feedback; the audience is not expected to take an active conversational role as in ordinary conversations. Of course, the audience may enter into a more active role if the speaker allows discussion or questions or indicates that a response is expected from the audience. However, even this conversational activity is generally restricted in length, content, and function.

The primary focus for speaker and audience is the delivery of the speaker's message. Lectures, for example, are conducted according to goals that are both informational and social. Although lectures do not require interaction in the form of talk, good lecturers are aware of the audience's need both to follow the flow of the talk and to enjoy the experience of listening (Goffman 1981). Therefore, speakers add features of discourse that, first, guide listeners in interpreting the information that they are hearing and, second, create interest in the content and involve the audience in sense-making. But, in general, they do not interact at the level of being reciprocal conversational partners with the audience.

Interpreters in this interaction must also focus on transmitting the content of the talk. Because of this, their role is generally viewed as passive in the same sense as the role of the audience is seen as passive. In fact, their role is more active than has been described in most accounts. Interpreters and those who study their work tend to focus on the transfer of the message contained in the words and sentences. This focus tends to exclude discussions about levels of meaning used to create audience involvement and levels of meaning derived from discourse structure and style. But these levels are important when producing target language equivalents because they contain cues that tell listeners what kind of message they are hearing, how to identify salient points in a message, and how speakers are projecting their involvement with the audience (Goffman 1981; Tannen 1989; Roy 1989b).

Defining interpreted events is different from using an interactionistic analytical framework to answer certain questions about interpreting.[1] Interpreting can be studied via a discourse framework regardless of the situation in which it occurs and the number of speakers that take part in it. For the purpose of definition, however, I am contrasting single speaker interaction with conversational interaction to suggest that such a definition offers students and practitioners a different vocabulary for talking about the dimensions of interpreting.

Conversational Interpreted Events

In discourse events, the direction and flow of talk and interaction are influenced by many factors. One of the most influential is the role participants are cast in for particular situations. Interpreters typically interpret in circumstances where primary participants are not coconversationalists (Goffman 1981), but whose concomitant roles and relationships are characterized at different levels. For instance, if the two participants are an employer and an employee, the employer may ask a greater number of questions, as well as different kinds of questions, than the employee can or is willing to ask. Then, factors such as status and authority, render the flow and character of the talk different from ordinary conversation.

In situations or events where interpreters appear, the participants are rarely equals. One participant usually has greater status or authority than the other participant by virtue of real or perceived status,or by the authority invested in a role, or by the participant's membership in the majority culture. The other participant is typically a member of a linguistic, ethnic or cultural minority and may be undereducated and/or underemployed. That is not to say that interpreters do not appear in situations where people are equals. For example, visitors to the United States from Russia engage interpreters to tour the country and meet Americans. However, these situations are clearly different and not as common as interpreted situations in which a European-American is talking to a Hispanic-American of immigrant or alien status.

For these reasons, the goals of conversation are multiple and individual to each participant. The purpose of a meeting as perceived by one participant may be vastly different from the purpose perceived by another participant. One participant may have come to a meeting to complain, and the other may have come to avoid accepting responsibility for a problem. Both of these participants may even have secondary reasons for meeting. The complaining participant may ultimately want leadership of the next project, for example.

Primary participants have specific interactional goals to accomplish, and conversation is the way these goals are achieved. For example, let's examine a meeting between a person a bank officer about a loan. For the person, the task here is to get the loan by convincing the bank officer of her trustworthiness and ability to pay back the loan. For the bank officer, the task is to make an evaluation of the borrower to be and to determine whether or not a loan will be made. So, as Goffman (1981) has pointed out, it is the accomplishment of this goal, or work as he terms it, that the conversationalists have as their chief concern, not the utterances: "One clearly finds, then, that coordinated task activity—not conversation—is what lots of words are part of" (1981: 143).

In addition to accomplishing a primary goal, speakers portray images of themselves–images perceived by others. The talk that emerges is not only about the task or goal at hand but is significant in the way participants signal to each other what is going on moment by moment and how to interpret those moments (McDermott and Tylbor 1983). Commands, apologies, compliments, and other speech acts underlie much of the meaning of the words that are said.

It is in these conversational, interactive events that interpreters, by the workings of conversation, must take on an active role in the exchange of talk. Consequently, defining these events along interactional dimensions assists researchers, students, educators, and examiners in examining and portraying the work of interpreting.

Boundaries of Interpreted Events

Interpreted events, constrained by interaction and participant roles, can be described then in terms of the features used to analyze any communicative event. Hymes (1974) noted that speech events are usually bounded; people know when the event begins and ends. In interpreting events, the boundaries are clear in two ways. First, interpreting events are bounded as any discourse event with a speech community—that is, most interpreted events are also the common events of a nation or society's cultural and institutional life. For example, a medical exam begins when the doctor enters and asks, "What's wrong?" or "What can I do for you today?" Just as this question forms the boundary of a medical exam for most Americans, it also acts as the same kind of boundary in interpreted events.

A second, yet important, way in which interpreted events are bounded is by the presence of an interpreter. The moment an interpreter is present, the event is different. If the interpreter leaves at any time, the event changes. The presence of an interpreter underscores whatever the specific event is. Thus, a medical exam becomes an interpreted medical exam.

Interpreters shape events differently for all the participants. For some participants, it is a relief to have an interpreter present so that all or a substantial part of the information is communicated. For other participants, it can be unusual, awkward, and, at times, frustrating or annoying to have an interpreter because their presence is intrusive and odd. Moreover, participants often switch between recognizing the interpreter's presence and ignoring the interpreter's presence, a disconcerting stance in addition to the requirements of the ongoing event.

Perhaps this discussion seems fairly obvious. However, it is common to read about interpreted events where the presence of the interpreter goes unremarked and where it is assumed that a discourse event proceeds as it would without an interpreter present. As research has demonstrated, the presence of an interpreter changes the event. Interpreting makes interaction possible; more important, the interpreter's presence alters the interaction by changing the expectations and assumptions that the primary participants have about the way such events proceed.

Describing One Interpreted Event

This study is based on the description and analysis of a single, inter-preted, videotaped meeting between a university professor and a gradu-ate student accompanied by an interpreter. As the researcher, I held the camera and recorded the meeting with a hand-held VHS camcorder. Fol-lowing is a brief discusssion about videotaping such an event, a rela-tively new research development, the analysis, and how the analysis is interpreted.

Videotaping Interaction

Interactive discourse events are rarely recorded because they are often personal and private. Consequently, to gain access to any private meet-ing, several factors play a role in allowing a researcher to tape such an event. For me, getting access to the meeting is directly attributable to my relationship with the primary participants.

I was a doctoral student at Georgetown under the direction of the professor.[2] The student and interpreter were both friends and col-leagues, and all are introduced further in Chapter 6. All three knew of my research and the need to capture an interpreted event on videotape. The student alerted me to the meeting and invited me to film it, knowing that all of us were acquainted and that it was a fairly routine meeting between a graduate student and a professor. All three agreed, generously, to the taping.

Recording people as they interact changes the way they interact because of what Labov (1972) calls the "Observer's Paradox." Linguists want to observe how people speak with each other when they are not being observed or think that they are not being observed. It was assumed that people changed their way of speaking once a researcher asked a question, listened, and recorded their speech. However, sociolinguistic research has shown that when people are involved in face-to-face interac-tion, the demand for their attention is so great that they forget that they are being recorded (Schiffrin 1994; Tannen 1984). Results with video-taping are similar. Although initially people may be nervous or guard their speech and actions when videotaped, if they have truly come to-gether to *do* something, to *talk* to each other for a purpose, then that interaction takes precedence and at some level, they "forget" that they are being videotaped.

A special note here because one of the languages involved is American Sign Language (ASL) which is visual. Deaf signers who are involved in programs where ASL is taught, where ASL research is conducted, where interpreting is taught, are frequently asked to be videotaped. When training interpreters, Deaf people telling stories or giving a talk are videotaped for students to practice interpreting. Interpreting students and practitioners themselves also are videotaped for evaluation and assessment. So both the student and the interpreter in this study are accustomed to being videotaped. However, they are accustomed to being videotaped for the purpose of language study or assessment, not for the purpose of research on natural interaction. It was highly unusual to tape both as they engaged in this meeting. They had never experienced being videotaped while engaged in an authentic, conversational event.

These participants gave me leave to videotape because the meeting was not overwhelmingly important, crucial, or personal. All three participants knew it was to be a short, simple meeting to discuss the student's assignment. Thus, none of the participants needed to be concerned about private or personal information becoming the subject of study and public scrutiny. As I mentioned earlier, although this kind of work is the bulk of interpreting work, most of it is very private, and most participants would be reluctant to have such a situation videotaped.

To underscore the importance of access, another interpreter attempted many times to get permission from primary participants and wa refused even though many of these meetings were seemingly inconsequential. Such is the reluctance of many individuals to allow a stranger to videotape their actions and analyze their language behavior.

The student, interpreter and I came together to the professor's office. As soon as we entered, I began taping. In taping an interpreted event in which participants use American Sign Language, the best of all worlds would be to use two cameras, one that captures a front view of the interpreter who sits next to an English speaking participant, and another camera to capture the front view of the student who is using ASL. In sign language interpreting, interpreters try to position themselves beside speakers who use English and across from speakers who use ASL. With only one camera and the interpreter as the crux of the communication, I stood behind and to one side of the Deaf student to film a frontal view of the interpreter. It meant capturing an over-the-shoulder view of the student. In this way, I filmed the student's signing but not his face. For this study, it was more important to know exactly what the interpreter was saying and doing.

Analyzing a Videotaped Interaction

The procedure for analysis, following Gumperz (1982) and Tannen (1984), was to transcribe what each participant said during the videotaped interaction. I wanted to describe how all three participants were involved, especially the interpreter. Because, at the time (1989), an interpreted event like this (only three people involved) had not been filmed or described in detail to my knowledge, it seemed best to begin with a basic feature of conversation, taking turns, determining when and how an exchange took place. After I identified the turns and discourse features surrounding turns, such as simultaneous talking and pauses, I grouped them into categories using the Sacks et al.(1974) descriptions of turns.

That accomplished, I turned to the three participants for playback interviews (Tannen 1984; Erickson and Shultz 1982). Playback interviews allow an analyst to replay an interaction for the participants (on an individual basis) and ask for their recollections of what they were thinking and their impressions of meanings. Obviously, these interviews need to be conducted soon after the original event before particpants' memories fade away.[3]

Playback interviews begin by showing the entire event to the participants. As Tannen (1984) notes, playback is a sensitive process. Interpreters in particular seem to assume that researchers are looking for mistakes. The explanation for this resides in their perception that they are continually confronted, both verbally and in writing, with their mistakes during interpreting. After asking the interpreter if he thought everything went smoothly and if this event accomplished its purpose from his perspective, which he did as did the other two participants, I explained that, because of the traditional tendency to criticize and find fault, my goal was to examine, describe, and explain this event in ways that described what good interpreters did as they interpreted. I was not looking for mistakes, rather asking how the interpreter made communication happen. Saying this, I gained his confidence and his openness in explaining his thoughts and actions.

After each participant has seen the entire event, I questioned each one about the event in general, getting their impressions of how it proceeded. As they watched again, I asked each one to pause if any instance was noted that impressed or bothered them in any way. In this way, the two primary participants began to talk about their general impressions of using interpreters. The interpreter talked about working as an interpreter. Finally, I played the tape again, asking them to watch particular turn exchanges and to comment on their own talk and actions, as well as on the talk and actions óf the other participants.

I directed the participants' attention to specific instances because in this brief meeting, each turn exchange happened quickly and other features, such as pauses or overlapping talk, were equally as brief. I had to show each segment several times, and as I showed them, I asked each participant first to concentrate on their own talk and actions. Then I rewound the tape and asked the participants to comment on the talk and actions of the other participants. Their observations, insights, and interpretations were crucial to my own analysis of the ongoing interaction, resulting in supplementing or adjusting the interpretations I had made.

Much interpreting research has been a comparison of the interpreter's output of the target language message with the original message. Typically, this results in categorizing interpreter errors—breakdowns that pinpoint the psycholinguistic stages of information processing. In short, pointing out what the interpreter has done wrong. My approach has been to adopt the perspective of studying an interpreted event which has apparently gone well by inquiring how such an event takes place, based on the understanding that successful communication requires a great deal of effort and energy on the part of all the participants, but especially on the part of the interpreter. More important, it is a study of the entire interaction.

Accountability in Analysis

Interpretive studies often come under fire as unobjective or unscientific because analysts arrive at interpretations of linguistic data. The charge is leveled that it is simply an analyst's supposition that certain meanings are created and sustained by participants within an interaction.

Tannen (1984) argues that interpretative studies account for their conclusions in three ways: there is (1) no single interpretation, rather multiple interpretations; (2) evidence from both internal and external patterns and accounts of interaction; and (3) the "aha" factor (37). Tannen proposes that one interpretation of an accumulation of data is not the only one possible, but rather others may draw different conclusions based on their focus and observations of activity. I offer my analysis is the same spirit.

Internal evidence is found in recurring instances of discourse features such that a pattern emerges. Then, such features are motivated in some way, not simply random. Although turns always occur in a conversation, there are differences in the ways they arise and how they transpire. Participant behavior is yet another example of evidence. When, in the interaction, I suggest that participants are acting or reacting in particular ways, then I describe the speech behavior or nonverbal activity that accounts for such actions.

For external evidence, I used playback interviews so that participants might share their feelings with me about the interaction, about talking to each other, and about what they could remember when taking a turn. Their reactions either confirmed or denied my analysis.

Tannen claims the "aha" effect occurs when people who hear a talk and read the explanation of behavior, exclaim within their heads, "aha!" When I've given talks about my study, interpreters around the country tell me "Yes, I do that, too!" I could not have better evidence for the interpreter's involvement or decisions in the interaction. Interpreters know that they are doing more than "just translating." They have not had the terminology to describe their activity within the process, but they know that the conversational interaction occurs much more smoothly when they intervene in these events. Tannen explains: "Most discovery, ultimately, is a process of explaining what is known. When the subject of analysis is human interaction—a process that we all engage in, all our lives—each reader can measure interpretation against his/her own experience" (1984: 38).

This chapter suggested a framework for the analysis of any interpreted event. First, I argued that the classifications of interpreting should separate along interactional lines. Second, I described a specific procedure and analytic method for investigating interpreted events. The next chapter is a description of the meeting place, provides a general summary of the meeting; and introduces the participants, their purposes for meeting, and their thoughts about interpreting and interpreters in their own words.

6

The Meeting and the Participants

Context

Social interaction is both composed of and composed by the interactants, their roles, their expectations, and their obligations within a social situation. Within interpreted events, getting to know the participants, their perspectives, and their reflections of what occurred is a luxury we do not have in real time. Not much has been written about the views or perspectives of the three people as they enter or emerge from an interpreted event. This chapter offers the opportunity to meet the three participants, to read their views about interpreters, to learn their goals within the event, and their reflections on being involved. This chapter sets the scene by describing the physical setting and an overview of the meeting. From this point on, I refer to the participants by their role titles as their names because it is their enactment, their assumptions and expectations, and their perceptions of their respective roles that are significant in understanding their words and actions. So, I introduce the Professor, the Student, and the Interpreter and allow their perspectives to come forth in their own words. In this way, they add to the definition, description, and understanding of the event we call interpreting.

The Meeting Scene

The three participants met on a fall morning thirty minutes before a scheduled class at the university. They met in the Professor's crowded office which was filled with bookshelves, filing cabinets, a desk, and two chairs. The Professor sat behind the desk, and the Student sat to one side of the desk. The Interpreter upended a trash can to sit next to the Professor, and I stood against the door and filmed.[1] The Student had come to a prearranged meeting thirty minutes before class was to begin. Thus, time was of the essence. The meeting had to be conducted as quickly, yet as thoroughly, as possible.

The Student was taking a graduate class in discourse analysis which focused on narratives that occur in conversation. The Professor explains the first requirement of the class: "The requirement for that class was that everybody tape record a conversation and choose one segment of it that they would then analyze for the whole semester. And a stipulation was that I had to approve." Students were expected to record several conversations, choose a narrative within one conversation, and transcribe it. During one of the first class meetings, they were to play the recording of the narrative and hand in a copy of the transcript for copying and distribution to the entire class. The Student recorded a story in ASL on videotape and requested a brief meeting with the Professor before class to have her approve it and to see if the transcription was acceptable in its present form. As with languages other than English, the transcript had to include both a literal translation (or gloss) and an idiomatic translation.

Student   Interpreter   Professor

The Meeting

An Overview of the Meeting

The meeting began as everyone sat down. The Student spoke first, beginning with an explanation of how he collected the narrative and transcribed it. Before he could say much, the telephone rang, and the Professor stopped the meeting to answer the phone. As she talked on the phone, the Student asked the Interpreter if filming had begun. The Professor hung up the phone, apologized for the interruption, and said that she would not answer the phone again. To do this, she had to adjust the telephone answering machine to answer the phone, yet silence the ring. As she went through these steps, she began to talk to the Student about the answering machine. When she was finished, she turned toward the Student, and the Student began to talk about using a TTY (a telecommunications device used in place of a telephone by Deaf persons) explaining how the light on the machine flickers and how he knows when the answering machine has answered the phone.

After a brief pause, the Student began to explain how the story came about, how the transcription and translation were accomplished, and then asked the Professor to approve the story. As the Professor took his paper, she explained that it was too late to arrange for a video machine to show his story in class that day but that she made the arrangement for next week. She began to read and read for approximately 80 seconds. When she finished, she looked up, said that the story was good, and began discussing it. Soon she introduced the topic of chunking (chunking is a way of parsing narratives into unified sections [Chafe 1980]). She discussed how chunks are recognized by linguistic and discourse cues in spoken languages and wondered aloud if ASL also has these cues. The Student replied that it seems reasonable that ASL would have these cues and suggested what they might be. The Professor replied that identification of these cues may take time and cautioned the Student to identify the chunks he recognizes in ASL, not in the translation.

As this topic came to a close, the Student asked if he could turn in the improved version for the class meeting next Wednesday (the class meets only once a week). The Professor asked for the finished version by Monday. The Student explained earlier in the conversation that he would be away all weekend giving a talk, so he mentioned again that he would be returning on Monday, implying that his paper would not be ready. After a brief pause, he offered to turn in his story on Wednesday, right before class. The Professor decided to see how many other students did not have their story ready and then decide what to do. The Student inquired if she wanted the version he has shown her or an improved one. She decided that students who did not have their stories ready that day should bring them to class next week with thirty copies (copies which will be distributed to other class members). The Student agreed to do that, and they began to close their conversation.

As they closed, the Professor asked the Student for phone numbers to reach him in the evening (something she requests of all graduate students). After a discussion of phone number, the meeting ended.

The Professor

The Professor, Deborah Tannen, is a professor of linguistics and a University Professor at Georgetown University in Washington, D.C. She is the author of numerous books and articles on discourse analysis, sociolinguistics, language and gender, and the connection between speaking and writing. She is most well known for her popular books: *That's Not What I Meant: Women and Men in Conversation*, which stayed on the bestseller lists for four years; *Talking from 9 to 5*; and, most recently, *The Argument Culture*. She grew up in Brooklyn, New York, attended graduate school in California, and now makes her home in the Washington, D.C. area. Before she attended graduate school, she taught English as a second language in Greece and speaks Greek.

My first questions were directed at her knowledge and experience with the other two participants. She knew the Student from his participation in a previous class: "I felt well-disposed toward him and comfortable with him in class. I've always liked [the Student] and I respected him too. I thought he was a good student, smart,and I always liked him." When asked what she thought about Deaf students in general, she replied that the first time a Deaf student had appeared in her class, she had been somewhat nervous, but now she has had four or five students in class over the years. She said:

> I like it; I mean I always found it interesting because we're in the business of studying language. Having access to that very different language, it's so instructive for us [professors at the university], it's good. And I suppose being hard of hearing I have a predilection to feel well-disposed for that reason too. I doubt it means much to them but . . . and they're right, from their point of view I can hear, you know, what does it matter but . . . but from my point of view I feel like there's a certain identity.

The Professor continued, explaining that as a teenager she had volunteered at the Lexington School for the Deaf in New York City. Noting the strong tendency of deaf children to sign even when forbidden, she retained positive feelings about sign languages as natural languages for Deaf people. She concluded, "So I had that background that made me feel well disposed."

As for the Interpreter, she had met him when he had interpreted classes from previous semesters. She had talked with him after classes and had liked him. When asked if she thought he was a good interpreter, she replied: "I think he is; I don't know why I think that, but I do. It's hard for me to separate my own sense of what he does and what I've heard about him. I seem to remember having heard he was a good interpreter . . . that he was a hearing child of deaf parents and that was really fluent in ASL." These comments led to asking if she felt comfortable using interpreters in classes. Her reply, as someone who is only slightly familiar with using interpreters, reflects anecdotal perspectives heard from participants who do not have contact with interpreters: "Yeah, but that's not to say that I'm not comfortable in the situation. My own hearing problem does create a special problem for me. It's that I compulsively watch people's faces when they talk because of being hard of hearing and it's really really hard for me not to look at the interpreter because I always look at people when they talk to me."

Although the Professor has a slight hearing problem which forces her to pay special attention to people's faces when they talk, the desire to look at the person who is speaking English is not an uncommon one, particularly with white (or European-American) listeners. In studying the listening behaviors of whites and blacks, Erickson and Shultz (1982) found that white listeners maintain a fairly steady eye gaze at speakers. When a Deaf speaker begins to use signs, participants who can hear attune to the voice of the interpreter, usually seated to one side. The Professor explains what many of these participants have told me: "You're supposed to look at the deaf person and it's counterintuitive—it's really hard to do." It is intuitive to look at the participant who is speaking, even more so when you begin to hear a language you understand. It seems reasonable that, in the first few moments, many of these interpreted encounters undergo a kind of interactional discomfort while participants figure where to look.

Conversely, participants who can hear discover another disconcerting aspect of talking with Deaf persons. Erickson and Shultz (1982) showed that many white American speakers, who do not gaze constantly at their conversational partners, gain a sense of the way the other is understanding their talk by returning to gaze at the listener fairly frequently. When these speakers check to see how a Deaf person is responding, they find that person looking at the interpreter. Imagine the discomfort of discovering that the listener is looking almost continuously at an interpreter (who is signing). As the Professor admitted, "It's a little bit like watching a movie with sound and the sound is off. It makes me uncomfortable." The Professor also admitted to an instinctive feeling that interpreters interfere with direct communication. She explains: "Yeah, they get in between. I don't feel like I'm communicating directly with them; I feel like there is an intermediary. I think I sense that I'm not receiving what they're saying directly, and I'm only mildly aware that a response is late at the time it's happening but I am aware that something's funny . . . but I'm looking at [the Student]. It's a strain."

This perspective, which does not prevent this Professor from having successful interactions with Deaf people, is rarely discussed in sign language or spoken language interpreting.[2] Perhaps because it conflicts with an interpreting belief system that attempts to persuade others that the presence of interpreters allows for direct communication. These comments are instructive and valuable in that they are from the point of view of the participant who is less familiar with using interpreters, as are many institutional representatives of the majority culture. In spite of her interactions with interpreters in the classroom and outside of the classroom and in spite of her successful encounters with Deaf persons, she articulates a perspective that should be noted.

The Student

The Student is a Deaf man in his late thirties who was an instructor at another university in the Washington, D.C. area.[3] At the time, he held a master's degree in linguistics and is actively involved in linguistic research on American Sign Language (ASL). He taught ASL and its structure to undergraduate students. He is also a poet and has performed his poems in many states.

He attended the Vermont School for the Deaf, a residential school for Deaf children through high school. Residential schools, which typically generate a negative concept for the majority of Americans, have the opposite connotation for Deaf persons. Residential schools are the places where Deaf children first acquire a natural sign language, meet Deaf adults, English speaking adults who sign, and become acculturated into the Deaf experience (Erting 1982; Lane 1984). Most Deaf adults retain strong ties with their former residential schools and identify themselves to newcomers in terms of the school they attended.

The Student has previously taken a class with the Professor. When asked if he'd met before with the Professor in her office, he could not remember for certain but said that meetings with a professor, doctor, or someone professional were not a new or strange experience. Having participated in interpreted speech events frequently gives him the advantage of experience; for the Student, meetings that include interpreters are the norm. He commented that the Professor was an interesting person, that her way of running a class was interesting and different, and that he felt challenged in her class.

Because it was early in the semester, the Student assumed that this was the first time to meet in the Professor's office. They had spoken using the Interpreter after a class meeting to ask a question. The Student volunteered his thoughts about people who speak English. He said that the hardest thing to understand is, "Well, their language, it seems hearing people have a strong tendency to be indirect. It's amazing and frustrating. For example, they say 'it's cold' and I know it means shut the window, but I had to learn that. I would say I'm cold and ask someone to shut the window. Hearing people [a term used by Deaf persons for people who hear and speak] just look at people and say 'I'm cold' and expect YOU to go and do something!"

It's typical in conversations with Deaf people for them to mention that people who use ASL "talk straight" and people who speak American English "talk in an unclear way." Deaf persons who use English in their everyday lives do so primarily through its written form or with a scrambled signed form neither of which adequately portrays the levels of indirectness found in spoken English. Much of the cross-cultural miscommunication that occurs between Deaf people and people who speak English arises from Deaf people misinterpreting when they are expected to understand indirect utterances conveyed through a sign language variety or through interpretation.

It seems a matter of general experience, including my own, that for years, interpreting was to convey a surface, or literal, rendition of English and subtle levels of indirectness had to be left for the Deaf speaker to interpret. This, of course, assumes a high level of fluency in spoken English, which would mean that Deaf persons need interpreters only to put spoken words into signed words.[4] As interpreting has professionalized and more is understood about the nature of language, indirectness becomes one of the difficult issues because the nature of indirectness lies in its ambiguity and deniability. By virtue of his studies in linguistics, the Student is able to comment on such indirectness, but he learns about indirectness through specific occurrences in his studies or through the experience of a specific utterance.

When asked about the Interpreter, the Student responded about selecting this particular person: [5] "He knows ASL; he's fluent; he's used it all his life, plus he's an experienced interpreter. He's interpreted classroom situations many, many times before. I feel that of all the interpreters, [the Interpreter] is the best. There are so FEW interpreters who know ASL, and he's the best. He understands me just fine."

Because Deaf persons have been subjected to varieties of signing that try to represent English, not all people who sign, including interpreters, use or are fluent in American Sign Language. These sign varieties can be difficult to understand, and graduate school is difficult enough without having to fight the problem of unintelligible language. Thus, fluency in ASL is a priority for the Student.

The Student also explained that this Interpreter had a "good attitude," a comment often heard from Deaf people who use interpreters. When asked what he meant by a good attitude, the Student replied that a good attitude included being flexible, supportive, and understanding and having knowledge and familiarity with Deaf culture: "Many interpreters tell me that they are proficient at ASL, but are they? I'm still learning ASL myself so how can they be proficient? It's just like English, you keep learning English, right? So telling me that they are proficient at ASL really turns me off." He continued by explaining that interpreters who have good attitudes acknowledge that they are still learning ASL, that they associate with Deaf persons, and show that they can be supportive. What then, I asked, is supportive? He responded:

> I feel that interpreters should side with Deaf people. If something goes wrong, it's usually that hearing people don't understand Deaf culture. Interpreters need to lean more toward Deaf people and make sure that things are working out. Yes, I feel that interpreters need to help, well, not help but add things that inform Deaf people about the ways of hearing people. When interpreters hear something and they know that the Deaf person is probably going to have a difficult time understanding it, then they should add information that explains things so that Deaf people get it.

That interpreters should side with Deaf people (a comment also heard by spoken language interpreters when working with minority speakers) is an issue outside the scope of this study. But it is an issue that resonates with interpreters and the words of Anderson (1976) about interpreter bias. Adding, subtracting, and changing a message are all possible in an interpretation and interpreters struggle with, for example, how much addition is needed and how much is too much? Which changes take responsibility from a speaker? It is these types of questions that a discourse perspective can answer by separating issues of communication and its process from issues of personal responsibility.

The Interpreter

The Interpreter was a young, white male in his late twenties who was pursuing a degree in anthropology at a university in an adjoining state. He was the son of Deaf parents, a graduate of an Interpreter Training program at Gallaudet University (an Associate of Arts degree), and was a popular interpreter in the area. He was certified at the highest level by the Registry of Interpreters for the Deaf, a national membership association of sign language interpreters.

He commented first on the Professor:

> [I think] she's very open to Deaf students. And she recognizes ASL as a separate language, a language in its own right. So that makes it good because some of her philosophies match with mine. She obviously has had experience with the interpreting process before. She's real comfortable with that, so that makes me more comfortable. As a teacher, I think she communicates better than a lot of teachers—clear, pacing is a little fast, but that's normal for her [but in class] there are always two interpreters, so that helps. She is also comfortable with interruptions, and that type of thing—that whole interpreting situation, she handled very comfortably.

The Interpreter's perceptions of the Professor's comfortableness is in stark contrast with her comments about the counter intuitiveness and slight strain of using interpreters.

As for the Student, he and the Interpreter knew each other personally and professionally. He has interpreted other classes for the Student and knows that the Student trusts him. I asked him why he thought the Student chose him as his interpreter: "[he selected me because of] the comfort factor, understanding, because I know ASL, and because of my attitude toward him and similar philosophies, and I don't know if it has anything to do with gender, but it's possible. And my commitment to the topic, I do the readings and we get together before class to discuss the readings." The Interpreter's remarks match closely with the Student's explanation for selecting this Interpreter. They both comment on fluency in ASL, attitude, understanding, and other qualitites. They are simpatico, and it no doubt works well for both. Their compatibility no doubt accounts for why both claim that the meeting went well. Understandably, the luxury of selecting an interpreter that closely matches one's stated preference is a unique occurrence in most interpreting events. For the most part, Deaf people have to accept interpreters who are available either by referral agencies or by their free-lance status.

Because this study is ultimately about an Interpreter's role, I asked the Interpreter for his perspectives on his role in face-to-face meetings:

> I'm not sure I see any difference between that and large group
> or, you know, audience kind of group, just to communicate, to
> convey one's ideas to another, and vice versa. Unless I'm
> called upon by either party involved and primarily both par-
> ties seem to agree then I get involved in a different level. You
> know, if there's some cultural mediation that needs to go on,
> it's really upsetting to both parties. Some things happen where
> people don't catch on right away, for example. If communica-
> tion gets messed up then I'll go whoa and stop everybody—
> 'you're talking to Janie and she is responding to you'—clarify
> or whatever, that's not culturally related.

The Interpreter's perspective that there is not much difference between three people and large groups because the point is "just to communicate, to convey one's ideas to another, and vice versa" is typical of how interpreters explain their job. Thinking in terms of interaction differences has not been part of the professional vocabulary or professional discussions for interpreters. Information and its correct conveyance remains a primary concern. Consequently, issues of communication, such as when a primary participant poses a question directly to an interpreter, are discussed as issues of ethics and power rather than about participant assumptions or expectations during conversational interaction.

As the Interpreter continues, he offers that he shifts his role when he is called upon to be involved. His example of involvement is when participants are not talking directly to each other, or clarifying who the speaker is and who the responder is, which again are communicative problems, not problems of culture. By the end of his comments, he has talked himself out of the idea that clarification of who is talking is cultural. Again, this is indicative of the lack of vocabulary and resources for talking about the subject matter that concerns interpreters the most, communication and its processes. There is a lack of descriptions and definitions for talking about the complex act of communication, especially when it's face to face. As the study of interpreting as a discourse process continues, and as we borrow terms and knowledge from the disciplines of language study, these terminology problems will disappear.

As the Interpreter indicates, interpreters are called upon to resolve communicative difficulties between primary participants. Good interpreters learn through experience which solutions work reasonably well and which do not. Managing communication is about making the process of talking across languages flow back and forth as smoothly as possible and with as little disruption as possible. It is simply a fact of life that most people rarely interact through an interpreter. They are not sure how the process works, and they assume that the interpreter is responsible for making it work. To do that, interpreters will have to acknowledge that they do more than "just translate" or "just interpret."

Participant Roles and Purposes

In talking about social situations and participants, Goffman suggests that situations move forward in accomplishing a goal or purpose because the participants come to a "working consensus" about the nature of the situation: "Together the participants contribute to a single overall definition of the situation which involves not so much a real agreement as to what exists but rather a real agreement as to whose claims concerning what issues will be temporarily honored" (1959: 9–10). The working consensus of most teacher-student meetings is realized through the expectations and obligations of the role of teacher and student. These roles have mirroring expectations (the actions others can insist we perform) and obligations (the actions we can insist others perform) (Goffman 1967: 126). For example, the obligations of the student role—to read, to take exams, to attend classes—are expectations of the teacher role. The expectations of the student role—to receive information, to be given fair exams, to be graded on the basis of merit—are the obligations of the professor role. Thus these roles become interdependent; the expectations and obligations are complementary and in service to each other.

In their interviews, both the Professor and the Student focus on the expectations and obligations of their respective roles as teacher and student. They both articulated the role of the Student as checking on an assignment (getting information) and making sure the Student had a clear understanding of the Professor's expectations (giving information). The Professor: "My view of the meeting was that I was there to answer [the Student's] questions, not that I was there to tell him anything. I think that's why I started the meeting by looking expectantly at him." The Student explained his purpose: "My purpose was to make sure I understood the assignment correctly and was going in the right direction. The paper was supposed to be handed in during class, and I held it back because I wanted her to check it first. If she approved, then fine, I would hand it in. I knew the ASL would be hard to understand, so I wanted to ask if I should go ahead with the ASL story or follow the English interpretation."

When asked if they thought the meeting was successful, that expectations and obligations were met, both responded affirmatively. They explain in their own words. The Professor: "The meeting was successful. Nobody yelled at anybody. [The Student] came to get information and he got it. The laughter, I think the laughter is my signal that everything is going well. I felt [the Student] knew what he was supposed to do." The Student: "She read my story and seemed satisfied with it. I knew she wanted me to improve it and bring it back with thirty copies. Yes, the meeting was successful." Although the Professor comments on the interactional success, "nobody yelled at anybody" as well, both speakers are attentive to the primary purpose, and their ensuing obligations, of a teacher-student meeting.

As the next chapter demonstrates, many of the Professor's and the Student's motivations for speaking or taking a turn center around their expectations or obligations of their social roles. Their roles define their purpose for meeting and constitute how they will interact and how their meanings are represented in talk.

The Interpreter's role is to interpret. In general, the role of an interpreter is to make possible communication between people who do not speak the same language. The Interpreter defined his role, what he says it always is, as working to have effective communication, "for people to communicate." However, when asked if he thought the meeting went well, he offered a perspective that was not centered around whether or not the participants had effective communication: "Yes, because I think [the Student's] goals were achieved, in getting some ideas across and talking about some issues. That he understood where she was coming from and she understood where he was coming from." Although this response is vague and unfortunately not further clarified, there are some indications as to what the Interpreter is referring. When the Interpreter mentions "[the Student's] goals were achieved," it appears that the Interpreter assumes goals other than getting an assignment reviewed. He continues by adding "getting ideas across" and "talking about some issues," but the only "issue" mentioned previously by the Interpreter is connected to people communicating. The Interpreter never mentioned checking the assignment or the Student getting information on how to analyze the narrative, nor did he mention the Professor's obligations she might have for meeting with students.

Because both primary participants are involved with the study of language and because the study of ASL as a natural language was still a relatively new idea, many conversations with linguists who study spoken languages come around to the topic of the differences between a signed language and a spoken language. At the time, the status of ASL as a language in the larger world community was not firmly established, nor was the status of Deaf persons as members of a linguistic and ethnic minority. That these "issues" particularly affect interpreters can be demonstrated by reading newsletters and journals published at the time in the interpreting field, as well as by attendance at meetings and conferences.

These debates and discussions are often referred to with phrases such as "getting ideas across" and "talking about issues," so I can suggest the possibility that the interpreter is referring to these potentially explosive arguments about the acceptance of American Sign Language as a natural language. Fortunately, this is not an issue with the Professor, as the Interpreter acknowledges: "She's obviously educated [about Deaf people] in that she's familiar with deafness and Deaf people because she explained the outgoing message on the answering machine, things that are very hearing culture and so I think that in some regards she took care of all that." Although he acknowledges that the Professor is familiar with deafness and Deaf people, it is also his focus on her adaptations to the Student that remain primary in his reflection on the interpreted event. The answering machine was a few seconds of small talk before the more important discussion of the Student's narrative and transcript.

The Interpreter's focus on "getting ideas across" and taking care of cultural differences reflects what is a central concern of interpreters in their role, the notions of equality and justice. It seems that the Interpreter feels that it is incumbent on him in his role to create an understanding and a balance between these speakers. Moreover, the Interpreter never commented on the discussion around the assignment for either participant.

To see how far the Interpreter's thinking was from the thinking of the primary participants, here is what the Professor said about the answering machine talk: "[I was] trying to be polite and make everyone comfortable, telling him about the answering machine and the knocking at the door and then I realized [there was] no reason to tell him." The Interpreter has attributed the meaning of the talk to the Professor's awareness of Deaf people when, in fact, she was focused on the nature of starting to talk and the often necessary small talk that is a prelude to official business.

Because interpreters are primarily concerned with communication, of language and also of cultural nuances, much of an interpreter's concern is for differences in language and culture. But speakers themselves are typically concerned with the central task of the meeting, carrying out their obligations and responsibilities necessary to accomplish their goals.

We will see in the next chapter that an interpreter's role is more than to "just translate" or "just interpret." What the role is and how to manifest that role to others, while appearing neutral or impartial, is not an easy task. If an interpreter's role expectations and obligations were as easily defined as the teacher or student role, then there would not be the problems, concerns, and issues that arise around the discussions about an interpreter's role.

7

Turn Exchanges in an Interpreted Professor-Student Conference

Turns

In professional discussions, papers, books, and pamphlets about interpreting, there is a largely underlying assumption that if speakers are talking back and forth, interpreters should make it possible for them to seem as if they are talking directly to one another. Although it may be possible at times for speakers to feel as if they are talking directly to each other, they are not. They are always exchanging speaking turns with the interpreter.

In interpreted conversations, just as in ordinary discourse, turns can be analyzed in terms of their structural characteristics. And, again as in ordinary discourse, some turns cannot be accounted for solely in terms of structural qualities. Some turns come about because participants take turns for reasons congruent with their roles. Turns are complex exchanges because, although the intent and content of a turn originates with each speaker, the interpreter has to allocate and manage the conversational exchange.

Turns are complicated entities because, upon hearing or seeing utterances whose meaning resides in other than linguistic form, interpreters have to make decisions from a range of possible choices. Choices have to include appropriate lexical and grammatical features, layered social meanings, possibilities for transition, and possibilities to elicit a response from yet another range of possible responses. Choosing an appropriate interpretation also depends on factors such as the relative status of the speakers and desired outcomes for the situation. For example, suppose a supervisor asks an employee this question: "Would you mind typing this for me?" Is this really a question or is it a "polite" request to type a paper? How immediate is this request? Interpreters have to select an utterance that may or may not be a question but must include the force of the request, the indirectness (if indirectness is appropriate in the other language), and a type that will elicit an appropriate response.

The analysis of the transcript revealed that turn exchanges are occurring between the interpreter and a primary speaker. Even though the content and intent of the turn originates with each primary speaker, the two speakers are not talking directly to each other in the sense that they are exchanging the direct surface signals of their respective languages. In interpreted events, speakers exchange speaking turns with the interpreter in their own languages. In this interpreted conversation, four categories of turns presented themselves: regular turns, turns around pauses and lag, overlapping turns, and turns initiated by the Interpreter.

It is also the case that phenomena around turns, such as pauses, lags, overlapping talk, and simultaneous turns, are going to occur naturally and as they are created by all three participants. The ongoing recognition of such discourse features are part of an interpreter's competence, and the resolution of discourse confusion, if necessary, belongs primarily to the interpreter.

Regular Turns

In this section, I present examples from the transcript of regular turns, or "smooth transitions" (Sacks et al. 1974). Regular turns in interpreting resemble regular turns in ordinary face-to-face conversation. The examples demonstrate how the interpreter and one or both speakers exchange turns and how a smooth, regular exchange in interpreting takes place.

At this point, let me say a few words about reading the transcript. The transcript is 253 line segments long. In the following examples, the number at the beginning of each line segments represents its place among the 253 lines. Within each segment, there is a line for each participant, the Professor (P), the Student (S), and the Interpreter (I). They are either speaking or are silent. American Sign Language is represented by all caps. English is represented by regular type. There is no transcription or gloss for the Student's ASL because the Interpreter provides a translation either within the same line or by the next line segment. Similarly, there is no gloss for the Interpreter's ASL because there is an English rendition immediately before.

Because ASL is not a written language and because grammatical relationships can be marked on the face, hands, and through movement and space, ASL is represented by glosses which are *literal* English representations of some *part* of the corresponding ASL lexical item. Therefore the meaning represented here is always somewhat skewed or simplified.[1]

Finally, I remind readers that the study has taken moments in real time that happened very quickly and has frozen them for a long, careful description and analysis.

A Regular Turn in English

In the following example, the Student has just finished a lengthy talking turn in which he explained how he got his narrative, and how he produced the English gloss of ASL and the translation. In line 60, he asks if the corpus he is analyzing is a narrative. The example begins with the Student's question, the Interpreter's rendition, and then the Professor's response.[2]

60
P:
I: write that down.
S: THAT-ONE STORY   NOT?

61
P:
I: I just want to see if you think this is a narrative.
S: (reaches for the folder, takes out paper, hands to P)

62
P: ┌Yeah. Ok great, uh
I: or not.┘
S:

63
P: I should say that I uh called up to get a VCR
I: FINE FINE   FIRST HAVE-TO TELL-YOU
S:

In this segment, a turn exchange occurs at line 62. As the Interpreter finishes his utterance "or not," the Professor begins speaking, "yeah ok great, uh." The turn exchange takes place between the Interpreter and the Professor; it is accomplished in the same language at a typical turn transition, a falling intonation indicating a stop (Duncan 1972). It is accomplished quickly with relative smoothness and without hesitations, lengthy pauses, or outward indications of a kink in the interactional rhythm. This is a regular turn.

The Student actually finishes his turn at talk with an ASL question (line 60). Although the Professor cannot and does not recognize this syntactic unit, she can see that the Student has stopped speaking (his hands are not signing) and is reaching forward for his paper. Until she hears the interpretation she cannot know whether this is a pause or an end to his turn. The Interpreter is the only one in the conversation who recognizes that a question has been asked in ASL, that the Student is finished, and that a finish in English must be signaled. The Professor recognized the indirect question and latches her response quickly to the end of the utterance constructed by the Interpreter (line 62).[3]

```
62
P:        ⌐Yeah. Ok, great, uhm
I: or not.⌐
S:
```

The Interpreter, then, has formed an utterance that is a lexical choice and has also chosen a prosodic cue for English which, in turn, produces a response. Interpreter translations are composed of more than lexical, phrasal, or syntactic choices. Choices of prosodic or paralinguistic cues are also required.

On the surface, the nature of this exchange is that, the Professor takes turns with the Interpreter. It makes sense that speakers take turns in relation to the linguistic utterance they understand. Thus, turn-taking as an organizational system of conversation occurs between the Interpreter and a primary speaker and between the Interpreter and the other primary speaker.

Why is it necessary to point out this seemingly obvious fact? Primary speakers in interpreted settings are often encouraged to think of themselves as speaking directly to each other. They quickly discover, however, that this is not the case and intuitively understand that they are exchanging turns with the interpreter. Doing so naturally and unconsciously suggests to speakers that they treat the interpreter as a direct interlocutor. It is no wonder, then, that often we find primary speakers addressing interpreters as participants who can answer questions and give responses. One can also understand how talking directly to an interpreter comes about; it is natural, even ordinary. Here, the transition from Student, to Interpreter, to Professor is a transition without problems. No one exhibits signs of being uncomfortable, nor is there any discourse muddle. A regular turn, then, can be labeled as such because of the naturalness and ease of transition.

A Regular Turn in American Sign Language

In the next example, the Professor is suggesting that the next step is to separate portions of the Student's narrative into chunks. She explains that narrative chunks in spoken languages are detected through linguistic cues, such as rhythm, intonation, and discourse markers (Chafe 1982). She concludes by saying that she does not know if ASL has these cues or if there are other kinds of cues. Her final remark, a rhetorical question, is interpreted into ASL as a direct question: Does ASL have cues? The Student immediately responds, "YES" (113).

113
P: I don't know if these exist or if there are others
I:　　　BUT PRO3　WHAT? NOT SURE HAVE #CUES? ⌐
S:　　　　　　　　　　　　　　　　　　　　　└ YES

114
P:
I: I-ask-you]#WHAT　　　　　　　　Yeah I'm pretty sure they
S:　　　　　　　　HAVE THINK SO

This example, too, is representative of a regular or smooth exchange of turns in interpreted encounters. Just as the Professor did, the Student latches his response immediately to the end of the interpretation (113). Again we have a turn transition across one language without hesitations, lengthy delays, or discomfort, and the exchange works smoothly.

As the Professor utters her rhetorical question (113), the Interpreter forms two direct questions in ASL, produced almost as quickly as the Professor speaks. When the Student begins to respond after the second question (HAVE #CUES?) and continues (114), the Interpreter produces an interpretation for the Professor in a relatively short amount of speaking time. The Professor's delay at hearing a response is minimal, less than a half second. The briefness of this delay accounts for the illusion that the speakers are almost talking to each other. Because the Student begins to respond in ASL by the second potential turn transition, the exchange between Professor, Student, and Interpreter occurs seemingly naturally within a brief time span and without problems.

That primary speakers are responding to the Interpreter in terms of the norms of their own language is also demonstrated by their nonverbal behavior. Both speakers nod their heads, smile and silently laugh, and make other gestures at moments that co-occur with utterances they understand in their own languages. For example, later in the meeting when the Professor learns that the Student will be going to another city to give a speech, she smiles and nods, but these expressions occur after she hears the interpretation in English, not after the Student says it in ASL. One wonders, then, whether the Student understands, intuitively or not, that the nonverbal information he sees the Professor engage in at that moment is attached to what he said moments ago. Brislin (1976) noted that when people speak the same language, they know what facial signals go with what words and so can interpret the combination of the two signals. But when we interact with people who speak another language, any speaker might observe another speaker's body and facial cues but most likely cannot associate these cues with their exact words, sentence, or meanings.

In this section I have demonstrated how the Student and the Professor take turns at potential transition moments within their own language, and thus, with the Interpreter. Regular turns occur naturally in face-to-face interaction, and they also occur naturally in interpreting. The participants, the discourse, and the moment combine (McDermott and Tylbor [1983] call this "collusion") to create interactional harmony whereby a turn happens successfully and comfortably. In *regular turns*, then, the Interpreter is an active participant who constructed equivalent responses in terms of message content and also in terms of potential turn transition. Knowing when and how to signal turns or pauses is discourse knowledge and an indication of communicative competence.

Creating Turns

From studies of noninterpreted conversations, we know that speakers do not take turns or continue their turns only because they recognize a transition moment or a specific syntactic unit that allows for exchange. Bennett (1981) suggests that the structural regularities in discourse and a participant's understandings of the thematic flow of the discourse make turn units "considerably more *flexible*" (emphasis his) than the notion of turns created solely from structural surface signals.

Within conversations, participants create themes which unfold, diverge, and reconverge as the talk proceeds (Bennett 1981). Themes, comprised of individual and shared motives, feelings about the subject, and the meanings that are uttered direct conversational contributions. Turns, then, also come about through participants' intuitive sense of "now" being the right moment to speak, or take a turn.

After playing back the videotape of the meeting once, I asked the participants to focus on turn-taking. I asked them to recall, if they could, their motives and feelings around their turns, and why, in some places, they chose to speak. Predictably, their own reasons for taking a turn or continuing a turn were based in large part on their own sense of participation in the conversation and from a sense of wanting either to contribute to a theme or, in one case, to stop a theme. These developments are not predictable but are a part of conversational behavior. Moreover, the ways in which the interlocutors contribute to the flow constitutes an emerging pattern of conversational style (Tannen 1984).

For example, at one point in the meeting, the Professor began to talk even though she could hear an interpretation. During her interview, I asked the Professor about this segment. Her response was, "I probably just decided it [the Student's talk] was enough. I didn't especially want to hear the answer now. I just wanted to set it as a topic that would be interesting for him to think about and report on during the semester."

The Professor began to talk from her own sense of the direction of the conversation and her desire to have the Student think about the topic and not initiate a longer discussion at present. To steer the conversation in a different direction and perhaps head off a lengthy discussion, she took a turn from her own sense of needing to alter the theme of the conversation, not from a surface syntactic signal.

In another example, at the beginning of the meeting, the Student was looking at the Interpreter because the Interpreter was signing, and then he turned away from the Interpreter and looked toward the

Professor and the telephone and answering machine. He began to talk while the Interpreter was still interpreting, not at a potential transition moment in ASL. His turn, too, has to be motivated by reasons other than an approaching grammatical unit or paralinguistic signal.

When asked why he stopped watching the Interpreter and began to speak, the Student replied, "I knew where [the Interpreter] was going; I could sense the way his sentence would end. I wanted to see what she was doing to make the phone stop ringing." (This he had learned from what the Professor had just said.)

Discourse knowledge, real world knowledge, a sense of conversational direction, speaker intention, and many other factors motivate speakers to take turns. Although interpreters cannot always predict when a speaker will talk, they can become accustomed to the possibilities of change and that turns can occur at the least likely moments, or rather, at any moment. Primary participants are actively involved in creating and responding to turns, and, for all intents and purposes, make arbitrary decisions which must be managed by an interpreter. More significantly, these examples demonstrate that primary participants are active in the emerging nature and flow of talk as the interpreter directs and coordinates the exchange.

Turns with Lag: Silences and Pauses

In interpreted conversations, speakers experience and perceive natural kinds of silences and unusual kinds of silences which emerge directly from the interaction of an interpreted event. One unusual type of silence during an interpreted conversation can develop when participants hear or see unintelligible speech or watch a signed language. Silence can also occur, as it might in ordinary conversations, from personal or purposeful acts that interrupt conversation. Part of each person's conversational style is a tolerance for how much silence or lack of a response there can be. Its length or brevity is, of course, relative to each person's style. Silence, though, creates opportunities for talking and taking a turn.

A Natural Silence

The meeting has just begun when the Professor's phone rings. After she answers it, she decides to set her answering machine to answer the phone so that she will not be interrupted while talking to the Student. Although the Student and the Interpreter speak while she performs that task, there are several moments when all three are not speaking, a kind of silence that could happen in noninterpreted conversations. Later, another silence develops when the Professor is reading the Student's transcript. While she does that, the Student and the Interpreter do not talk. These sorts of silences are natural silences that occur in ordinary discourse events.

These silences are potentially interesting because the possibility exists for the interpreter and one speaker to talk. Most training programs advise interpreters not to initiate conversations and to discourage speakers who want to initiate a conversation. But speakers with or without experience in using interpreters quite naturally perceive an opportunity to talk while the other human being in the room is occupied. This interpreting "rule" was created to keep novices from becoming full participants in an interpreted conversation and to help the two primary participants clarify that this is not an occasion to have a conversation with the interpreter. But, in practice, when such silences occur, the primary participants might initiate talk. As Metzger (1995) has pointed out, the lack of response from an interpreter could seem detrimental and unfriendly to the interaction rather than competent and professional.

Pauses Created by Participants

A pause, another kind of silence, is created by primary speakers, indicating their intention, after a few moments, to say something more or that they immediately think of something else to say. In this example, the Student indicates his desire to stop and think and then continue by using a gesture I call "wait-a-minute." This gesture, the index finger held up, palm side toward other speakers is a widely used gesture for getting other speakers to hold their turn.

171
P:
I: ok   all right
S: nod   #OK   **wait-a-minute** (looks at floor)

After this signal, all three participants are silent for an entire line segment afterward. Although there is no interpretation of this gesture, it is entirely within reason to assume that the Professor understood the gesture and, accordingly, waited for the Student to continue talking.

  In another place, the Professor indirectly asked for a minute to think and the Interpreter created a pause for her by using the gesture "wait-a-minute."

194
P: You know what?
I: this or you want this one? to put in?
S: points-at-paper------------------------------------

195
P: You know what I'm thinking, (hand over eyes)
I: with the group? or   **wait-a-minute**
S:

  As the Professor says, "You know what I'm thinking," with an intonation that signals "more to come," she looks down and covers her eyes with her hand. The interpretation of this utterance and its intonation is "wait-a-minute." As participants pause by indications within their own talk and nonverbal actions, the Interpreter assists in creating such pauses by gesturing "wait-a-minute." Again, the primary speakers are producing features of discourse, such as silence and pauses, and the Interpreter makes choices as to how those pauses are represented.

Regular Lag

In simultaneous interpreting, an interpretation *lags*, or is delayed, several seconds behind a primary speaker's message; this is *regular lag*. Especially when one of the languages is a signed language, this lag can create an unusual silence for the other speaker because while there is signing, there is no vocal noise. With two spoken languages, one speaker hears unintelligible speech.

  Regular lag can be found in two places. One instance occurs at the beginning of a speaker's talk whereby an interpreter does not begin to interpret immediately but starts a few moments later. Another instance occurs when one speaker's stream of talk ends, the interpretation continues, and then stops. A "next" speaker can begin several moments later (Sacks et al. 1974), and a lag is created while the first speaker either hears or sees talking and waits to hear or see an interpreter. This is ordinary and what interpreters mean when they talk about lag.

But regular lag also includes a perception by primary speakers that the delay in receiving an intelligible message is acceptable. The delay might be a half second, one or several seconds, or perhaps a full minute which results in a kind of silence unique to interpreted events. Regular lag assumes that speakers are not "uncomfortable" and that waiting for a response is acceptable.

However, waiting to hear an intelligible response can also put primary speakers on notice that this is an unusual communicative event. To a speaker who lacks experience with interpreters, it is reasonable to assume that these delays could be more disconcerting that to a speaker who is accustomed to using an interpreter.

Lengthy Lag

From regular lag, another type of lag can develop—a delay that becomes too long for one of the speakers. *Lengthy lag* occurs when a speaker perceives that the ensuing verbalizing or silence is taking too much time and reacts verbally or nonverbally. Typically this produces one of two results. The speaker who is uncomfortable begins to talk again, creating a pause, or exhibits some discomfort while waiting.

In this example, which occurs moments after the meeting begins, the Professor explains that she scheduled a TV/VCR for next week's class to show the Student's ASL story.[4] After waiting one second, while the interpreting occurs, the Professor begins to speak again.

65
P: They couldn't schedule it so I scheduled it for next week.
I: TODAY RESERVE?   [It's] TOO-LATE SAY SORRY CANT
S:

66
P:
I: MEAN   TODAY CAN'T   NEXT-WEEK CAN   #OK?
S: (hd nod)

67
P: for showing in class.
I: CAN DURING CLASS SHOW PRO3 TODAY CAN'T
S: (hd nod)   (hd nod)   (hd nod)

68
P:
I: SHOW   BUT NEXT-WEEK   Ok   that's fine
S: FINE (repeat)   #SURE

The Professor speaks one utterance (65) and pauses (66). Meanwhile, an interpretation into ASL is produced which lasts one line segment (a full second), and then the Professor speaks again (67). Later, in while viewing this portion on videotape, she indicated that she continued for a reason: "I'm waiting for a response, and it doesn't seem to come, so I say something." The lag becomes lengthy, not because of a time count, but because of the Professor's perception that the ensuing silence lasts too long.

One of the factors that may have prompted the Professor to continue talking is that, after the interpretation, the Student begins to respond by nodding his head. As the Professor finishes in line 65, she hears nothing for a full second, although it is possible that she sees the interpreter signing. This lack of any speaking may have increased the perception of silence (or that there might not be a response) by the Professor. The Professor's wait for a response in this example becomes important in the light of future silences.

The next example of a lengthy lag, a segment that occurs near the end of the meeting, is when the Professor waits but signals her discomfort nonverbally. Interestingly, however, she continues to wait without adding more talk. The Student wants to hand his paper in at a later date. The Professor wants to see if other students in the class are finished with their transcripts the following week rather than today.

187
P: If there's a problem for a fair number of people
I: ME   TODAY ASK-SEVERAL-PEOPLE THAT SEE
S:

188
P: Then we'll put it off a week.
I: HOW-MANY PEOPLE   PRO3   DON'T HAVE (neg)
S:

189
P:
I: THEN MEAN "WELL" ONE-WEEK   POSTPONE
S:

190
P:
I: #IF PRO3 DON'T HAVE (repeated)   "WELL" WAIT
S:

191
P:
I: #IF ALL   HAVE   CAN GIVE-ME MONDAY?
S:

192
P: (turn and look at I, turn back to gaze at S)
I: COPY   ADD-TO-GROUP gesture
S:

193
P:
I: Ok, uhm   so I should improve
S: SAME-AS THAT?   point to paper CHANGE-SLIGHTLY   point

After two line segments, the Professor is finished. The Interpreter is interpreting from what was said before and continues interpreting for the Professor. The Interpreter actually starts interpreting this segment on line 187 and continues for six lines. The interpretation continues on and on while the Student says nothing and the Professor says nothing. At line 192, after waiting for three and a half lines or transcript or more than three seconds, the Professor turns, looks at the Interpreter, and then looks back to the Student. Her movement and her facial expression seem indicative of a sense of puzzlement, but she does not initiate any talk and continues to wait for a response. I consider this another example of lengthy lag because of the discourse time that elapses and also because of the discomfort displayed by the Professor.

It is not hard to note examples of lengthy silences during which primary participants display uneasiness. In her interview, the Professor commented several times that because she heard no response in what seemed to her a reasonable delay, she continued talking. This can be attributed to her own conversational style of faster pacing and pausing discussed in her book *Conversational Style: Analyzing Talk among Friends* (Tannen 1984). More interesting, however, is that her tolerance for a reasonable delay grew from a length of two clauses to five clauses, or from one second to slightly more than five seconds.

Learning about Lag

From studies of ordinary discourse we know that although participants begin to talk in a context, they continue to contribute to contextual features, changing the context as the interaction proceeds (Goffman 1981; Gumperz 1982; Schiffrin 1994). In so doing, they learn how to interact with their conversational partners. Thus, it is not unique to learn that primary speakers who lack experience with interpreters seem to learn about interpreted interaction as they progress through a meeting. However, it is unique in the sense that this learning, for the most part, remains undescribed and unaccounted for.

In this meeting, the Professor "learns" how interpreted conversations proceed so that her tolerance for lag and her wait for a response grow, gradually increasing in length. At the beginning of the meeting, she turns several instances of lag into pauses by speaking again. As the meeting continues, she tolerates longer periods of silence but still turns these delays into pauses. Later, she accepts another long silence which the Student changes into a pause to shift to a new subtopic. Toward the end of the event, she waits for a response even when it becomes longer than she normally tolerates.

Here are segments of talk demonstrating that the Professor is learning about lag through the course of the event. The first example has already been presented as turning lag into a pause by adding more talk (67).

65
P: They couldn't schedule it so I scheduled it for next week.
I: TODAY RESERVE?   [It's] TOO-LATE SAY SORRY CANT
S:

66
P:
I: MEAN TODAY CAN'T   NEXT-WEEK CAN   #OK?
S: (hd nod)

67
P: for showing in class.
I: CAN DURING CLASS SHOW PRO3 TODAY CAN'T
S: (hd nod)   (hd nod)   (hd nod)

In this example, the Professor waits for one full line or one second and
then begins to talk again. The next example occurs after 77 lines of
transcript, during the Professor's discussion of chunking cues. She explains that Chafe (whose article the students read for class) suggests that
these chunking cues result from speakers focusing on one piece of information at a time and, if that is true, there must be a corollary in ASL. The
Professor stops and waits for an interpretation, and then before she actually hears something in English, she speaks again.

144
P: If there isn't, that would disprove him.
I: THAT   #IT IDEA SUPPOSE
S:

145
P: (laugh)
I: #IF NOT ZERO-PRO3
S:

146
P:
I: THEN MEAN #HE #CHAFE WRONG   "WOW" gesture, shrug
S:

147
P: (wave hands)   Probably there is
I: No I doubt
S: ME DOUBT ME

In this example, she waits for the delay caused by the interpretation for
two and a half lines of transcript before she speaks again. During this
sequence she waits but, in the last line of this example, speaks again
before she hears the interpretation of the Student's response (147).

　　　During her playback interview, she felt that she spoke because
she had more to say. "I thought I was finished and then I decided I wasn't
finished." I asked her if the silence bothered her or prompted her to say
more. She replied that she did not think so, and, on seeing the sequence
again, she felt that she had been finished when she said, "that would
disprove him." She spoke again in line 147, "Probably there is" because
she had more to say. In this example, then, the toleration for interpreting
lag is growing. Thus, two and a half seconds has become acceptable
while waiting for an interpretation and she does not exhibit any signs of
discomfort, a contrast from the previous example.

　　　Another 35 lines later, the Professor waits for an interpretation
which continues for five lines of transcript. This sequence occurs after
the Professor explains about collecting transcripts, copying them and
distributing them. As she completes the last part of her talk (188), the
Interpreter has begun interpreting. His interpretation continues for five
lines. After the third line, or three seconds, the Professor shifts in her chair,
turns her head, looks at the Interpreter, and then looks back to the Student, all without saying a word.

188
P: Then we'll put it off a week.
I: HOW-MANY PEOPLE   PRO3   DON'T HAVE (neg)
S:

189
P:
I: THEN MEAN "WELL" ONE-WEEK   POSTPONE
S:

190
P:
I: #IF PRO3 DON'T HAVE (repeated)   "WELL" WAIT
S:

191
P:
I: #IF ALL   HAVE   CAN GIVE-ME MONDAY?
S: `

192
P: (turn and look at I, turn back to gaze at S)
I: COPY   ADD-TO-GROUP gesture
S:

193
P:
I: Ok, uhm   so I should improve
S:SAME-AS THAT? point to paper CHANGE-SLIGHTLY point

Here the Professor's wait for a response is remarkably long. As she watched this particular segment of the meeting, she remarked, "If I'm really going to have to wait this long, I'll just settle in here." From the beginning of this meeting to the end, the Professor has extended her ability to tolerate the delay of lag, adjusting her acceptability of how much time she must wait for a response.

I include this discussion because it demonstrates yet another way in which primary speakers are involved in this exchange. Their participation, intentions, and responses enormously influence the nature of this discourse process. More important, as the section has shown, primary speakers, while participating as they normally would, also "learn" how to interact in interpreted events.

Overlapping Talk and Turns

In face-to-face interactions within one language, when a speaker decides to talk, she can do so at almost any moment in the talk of another speaker. Thus, the potential exists for any one speaker to talk when a current speaker is already talking. Although many linguists have called this "interruption," Bennett (1981) pointed out that when two people talk at the same time, the description of what is happening is *overlap*, whereas *interruption* is a judgment regarding individuals' rights and obligations when speaking. Overlapping talk is not always nor consistently viewed by speakers as interruption (Edelsky 1981; Murray 1985; Tannen 1989). Many American speakers, women for example, tolerate overlapping speech without labeling it interruption (James and Drakich 1990).

The term overlap, or overlapping talk, includes both brief spurts of talk and talk which could continue for longer. Instances of overlap include everything from brief listening responses, to indications of understanding or the lack of it, words of agreement or disagreement, and when two speakers begin talking at the same time.

In simultaneous interpreting, one kind of overlapping talk is constant—interpreters talk as primary speakers are talking. This kind of simultaneous talk of speaker and interpreter, which, in face-to-face interpreting, can be seen or heard by all participants, is a marker of the unusual nature of an interpreting event.[5] This interlingual overlap becomes an accepted norm of these face-to-face encounters and is not the kind of overlapping talk discussed here.

However, another kind of overlap occurs in interpreted encounters which requires the interpreter to intervene. This is the overlapping talk that occurs between the two primary speakers.[6] This overlap can easily be understood because two participants can begin simultaneously, respond to another's talk briefly or at length, ask a question, exclaim, and so on. This is not to say that overlapping talk by primary speakers is customary. In fact, it appears that, for the most part, participants in an interpreting situation are aware that something unusual is going on and adjust their usual habits of talking—that is, they are more cautious about taking a turn, and, many times, are never sure when it is their turn.

Overlapping Talk and Choices

In any language there can be overlapping talk by speakers without noticeable disruption of interaction. But overlapping talk between two speakers in an interpreted meeting forces an interpreter to act. An interpreter cannot interpret two speakers at the same time; thus overlapping talk during interpreting has an impact different from when it occurs in ordinary conversation. When it occurs, two things are immediately apparent: (1) the possibility exists for *three* people to be talking; and (2) the interpreter must make a decision. Then the question is, What does the interpreter do, or rather what choices are available to the interpreter?

The options presented here are not exhaustive, but represent the possibilities seen in this study and from personal experiences. The point is that when interpreters mediate communication, they have choices and can make decisions. These are possibilities when overlapping talk occurs:

1. An interpreter can *stop* one (or both) speakers and allow the other speaker to continue. If an interpreter stops both speakers, then either the interpreter indicates who speaks next or one of the primary speakers decides who talks next.
2. An interpreter can *momentarily ignore* one speaker's overlapping talk, hold the segment of talk in memory, continue interpreting the other speaker, and then produce the "held" talk immediately following the end of a speaker's turn. Decisions about holding talk in one's memory lie within the interpreter's ability to do so and the interpreter's judgment regarding the importance or impact of the talk to be held in memory.
3. An interpreter can *ignore* overlapping talk completely.
4. An interpreter can momentarily ignore overlapping talk and upon finishing the interpretation of one speaker, *offer the next turn* to the other speaker, or indicate in some way that a turn was attempted.

Stopping a Turn

To stop a speaker, an interpreter has to do something, verbally and/or nonverbally, within microseconds of the overlapping talk. Although there may be several strategies in any language for stopping a speaker, interpreters also have to consider other factors, such as message importance, speaker relationships, and relative status or authority. Inevitably, interpreters have to choose strategies that work in specific situations with specific speakers. Because of the nature of interpreting employment, it is not unusual for interpreters to work in situations where they do not know the speakers or know them only slightly. This forces interpreters to learn the factors of a situation quickly. Thus, interpreters must know a wide range of communicative strategies and, as they learn about interlocutors—just as interlocutors learn about participating in an interpreted event—they make decisions about which strategies to use.

This example is particularly rich with three instances of overlapping talk between the primary speakers. Two instances of overlap are within the first seven seconds of this segment, brief, and practically imperceptible. The third instance, however, is more dramatic. As three people begin to talk, the Interpreter has to do something.

The first overlap occurs as the Professor begins a new topic. She has been discussing why the Student's work is good but needs some corrections. Then, with almost no hesitation, the Professor switches to a new topic, "chunking."

99
P: Ch- ⌉ Chunking
I: ⌉ Yes, I agree.
S: YES ⌋

100
P: I have no idea how   ⌐Chunking (laugh)
I: #CHUNKING   PRO3 (shrug) |
S: SAME (shrug)   └#CHUNKING (laugh)

101
P: So that's gunna be a very interesting ⌐
I: Yeah that's gunna be an issue Uhm I don't either⌐ **wait-a-minute**
S: KNOW   PRO1 NOT YET   UNDERSTAND⌋ HOW

102
P:
I: TRUE INTERESTING
S: USE

103
P: That's gunna be a very interesting thing for you to work out
I: DEPEND   REAL INTERESTING
S:

At the beginning of this segment, "YES" is the Student's response to the Professor's previous utterance. As the Student says "YES," the Professor simultaneously starts her new topic with "Ch-" but doesn't complete the word. This is the first instance of overlapping talk as the Professor and Student both utter together. Both contributions are brief; the Professor doesn't even finish her word so there is no need to stop them. The Professor appears to hear and understand the "Yes, I agree" rendered by the Interpreter.

  The second overlap occurs one line later when the Professor and the Student say "chunking" together. The Interpreter has let the Student know that the Professor is talking about chunking, and as the Professor says, "I have no idea how," she sees the Student shrug, look puzzled, and shake his head. Although she pauses briefly, as she says, "chunking" again, so does the Student. As they say "chunking" together (100), they both see each other speak, and they laugh together briefly. Again, it seems a spontaneous occurrence, brief and ending quickly.

These first two instances of overlap happen quickly and without need for a resolution. Then, a third instance of overlapping talk begins, all three are talking, and the has to intervene. (101). The Student offers back-channel responses, the Interpreter begins translating and then the Professor begins to speak.

101
```
P:          So that's gunna be a very interesting  ─┐
I:      Yeah that's gunna be an issue  Uhm I don't either─┤  wait-a-minute
S: KNOW     PRO1 NOT YET          UNDERSTAND ─┘  HOW
```

Suddenly there are three speakers. For a moment, all three are talking. And, at this point, the Interpreter says "wait-a-minute" to the Student.[7] The Student immediately shifts his gaze from the Professor to the Interpreter. As he sees the gesture, the Student's hands go down to his lap, a

Student   Interpreter   Professor

"Wait-a-minute"

turn-ending signal in ASL (Baker 1977), and he makes no further attempt to speak. When the Student stops, the Interpreter begins interpreting for the Professor, and she goes on talking.

At first glance, it might seem that the Interpreter stopped the Professor merely because she is the teacher and therefore more powerful while the Student is a student and thus powerless. But as Tannen (1987) argues, the notion of power is metaphoric when applied to interaction and discourse: "I suggest that there are many different kinds of power and influence that are interrelated and have varied manifestations. When people are taking different roles, it may not be the case that one has power and one doesn't, but that they have different kinds of power, and they are exercising it in different ways" (5). While the Interpreter may had made his decision based on greater authority or status of the Professor, upon closer inspection, a number of factors may have contributed to the Interpreter's decision to stop the Student.

First, the topic was initiated by the Professor, and it is clear that she is not finished talking about it, given her persistence in raising it and her elaboration of it. Second, when the Professor begins to talk about chunking, she says this word the same way both times. There is stress on the first syllable, as well as a rising and then falling tone. When said as "CHUNKing," in English, the tone carries an additional message of "here's what I want to talk about next." This is an example of how contextualization cues work (Gumperz 1982). Third, in playback interviews, the Professor and the Student explain their perspectives on the overlapping talk and the Interpreter's choice. The Student began explaining when he saw himself sign "SAME." The Student: "I said 'SAME' because I wanted to talk about the same thing! Chunking, and I was glad she brought it up. I didn't really understand it and hadn't remembered to ask her about it. I wanted her to talk about it." At some level the Interpreter knew that the Student needed to know what the Professor thought; it is what all students come to professors to hear. Although, by virtue of the situation, the Professor has a more powerful status, the Student's own words make it clear that he would prefer to be stopped, so that he can fulfill his expectation of receiving advice and information. It is for this information that he came to her office.

The Professor explains her perspective: "When I'm talking about chunking I think I clearly feel that what I have to say takes priority. And I want to get it out. [The Interpreter] starts talking but I don't want to hear it. I think I'm not sure whether [the Student] was trying to take a turn or give a back channel but I'm going to treat it like a back channel because

I want to keep talking. I wasn't ready to yield the floor." Thus, the Professor was unwilling to give up her turn and perhaps would have insisted that she be allowed to go on speaking. The accumulating data—her persistence on the topic, her contextualization cues, and her status—become a cumulative force that must have had some impact on the Interpreter's decision. Thus, in some ways, the Interpreter's decision was not only a judicious one to make; it was, perhaps, the only one the Interpreter could have made as part of this triad.

Overlapping talk and the decision to stop a speaker come about for complex social reasons within specific contexts and interpreters act instinctively on this knowledge.

Ignoring a Turn

Next, I move to examples of overlapping talk where the Interpreter makes a decision either to momentarily ignore one speaker's overlapping talk and interpret it later or to ignore the talk altogether. Momentarily ignoring a turn forces the Interpreter to "hold" a span of speech in memory (if able) until an opportunity presents itself to interpret what was said. Holding a span of speech and recalling it later happens for several reasons: (1) an interpreter perceives that the talk is not critical at the moment; (2) the overlapping talk is short, simple, and easy to remember; or (3) an interpreter can predict that one speaker is either finishing or will finish soon. When interpreters ignore a speaker's input, they generally do so because they decide that the talk is unimportant at this moment, that it may be contributed again, or that they simply cannot process that piece of language while they are interpreting.

In this segment, at the third line, the same occurrence that made the Interpreter stop a speaker previously now has a different outcome: the Professor speaks, the Student speaks, and the Interpreter is interpreting; all three are speaking (143). This time the Interpreter does not render an interpretation of the Professor's talk.

141
P: And I would guess that there is
I: PRO3 USE-SIGN   HAVE   #TOO TRUE
S:

142
P:
I: ME GUESS FEEL OTHER HAVE
S:　　　(Nodding)　　　　　　#YES

143
P: But if there isn't
I: Yeah,　me too (very softly)
S: FEEL SAME

144
P: If there isn't, that would disprove him.
I:　　　　　　　　　THAT　　　　　#IF IDEA SUPPOSE
S:

In this example, all three participants overlap (143). The Interpreter interprets the Student's contribution, but does not interpret the
Professor. One reason that suggests itself is that the Interpreter's experience with her conversational style suggests that she will start anew. Experience in this conversation alone has proven that the Professor will persist
in what she has to say. The Student's contribution is of a back-channel
nature, brief, and does not necessarily mean that he wants a turn. Notice
that the Interpreter interpreted the Student, not the Professor.

Interpreters sometimes have to ignore one of the overlapping
utterances. There are two kinds of talk that they can ignore and not affect
the outcome too drastically. One kind of talk is back-channel responses,
brief spurts of talk that indicate that listeners are paying attention, or
agreeing, or providing other noncontent responses, such as, "mm-hmm,"
"sure," or "OH-I-SEE (ASL)."

The other kind is also brief but contains more message content.
For instance, "yes, I can do it" and "no, I doubt it" are brief, yet they
include agreement, disagreement, or a proposition. Interpreters can, or
have to, ignore these two kinds of talk for two basic reasons. First, it is not
physically possible to hear or see two speakers and be talking yourself,
all at the same time. The complexity of the talk that is being interpreted
demands an interpreter's full attention. Second, inserting overlapping
talk could surprise the speaker who is already talking and that speaker
will stop because the stream of thought is interrupted.

The next segment demonstrates more of the unique possibilities
of interpreted events. The Student responds to something the Professor

has said, and his response is not interpreted. The Professor sees the Student make a gesture that gives agrees with her message, and it seems to communicate directly with her.

```
82
P: Ah, somebody's knocking at the door, by the way
I:                      PERSON        KNOCK #DOOR
S:
```

```
83
P: let's just ignore them (gesture)
I:        INFORM-YOU
S:                  (Point at door, gesture)      LEAVE-ALONE
```

```
84
P:
I: TRUE            IGNORE          LEAVE-PRO3      (gesture)
S:                                      OK
```

As the segment shows, the Student's contribution at line 83, pointing at the door, making a gesture as if to wave off something, and LEAVE-ALONE, is not interpreted (at line 84 there is no interpretation into English). The Interpreter had relayed the knock on the door, and it appears that the Student's gestures and perhaps facial expressions convey a sense that he understands her suggestion and nonverbal hand motions to ignore the knocking. Interpreters do not always interpret everything. In each of these examples the Interpreter ignored something the Professor said and something the Student said. Further study of the kinds of utterances interpreters ignore can tell us more about interpreter decisions.

Finally, interpreters sometimes make decisions to ignore overlapping talk momentarily, and when they are ready to interpret, they no longer remember it. When this happens, interpreters have an option to offer a turn to the speaker whose talk was ignored. Interpreters can say something like, "Do you want to say something?" or they can take a turn to say that the other speaker tried to say something. For example, an interpreter might say "Excuse me, there's a question." In this meeting, the Interpreter does not ignore overlapping talk momentarily and offer a turn to one of the speakers. However, the Interpreter does offer turns at talk for reasons other than overlapping talk.

Decisions About Turns

Overlapping talk is a difficult dilemma for interpreters. Whether the talk is simply of a back-channel nature or will become an attempt to take a turn does not deny its potential meaningfulness in conversational activity. As overlapping talk begins, any prediction as to its eventual length is a fifty-fifty probability. In interpreted conversation, the only participant who can begin to comprehend the import of overlapping talk is the interpreter (who may also be the first to realize that overlapping talk is occurring). Acting on these communicative "problems," and acting on them quickly, is what interpreters do.

On what basis do interpreters make decisions about strategies such as stopping speakers, ignoring talk, and offering turns? Predicting how conversational activity will proceed is difficult, particularly when the participants are relatively unknown to the interpreter. The Interpreter in this study explained that most of the time he judges the purpose of a new utterance by simultaneously considering what has been said, who has said it, and what the topic is or by waiting until the first parts of an utterance are produced to see if he can predict its import or direction.

During this meeting the Interpreter consistently stopped the Student and never stopped the Professor. The Interpreter did not interpret the Student's contributions to the conversation four times. Many interpreters who are concerned, and rightly so, about the rights and equal treatment of minority speakers, might argue that the Interpreter did not act appropriately or was acting in a way that oppressed the Student. However, conversations with the Professor and Student suggest that issues of equality and rights were not among their priorities. The Student chose this Interpreter because of his fluency in ASL and his attitude. As I discussed previously, the Student had come to the Professor for advice and assistance and was glad that the Interpreter had stopped him. He wanted to hear (see) what the Professor had to say. The Professor was concerned about evaluating the narrative, discussing the idea from class, and getting copies of the narrative to other students. Under the constraint of time and the knowledge that other students were waiting to see her, she did not want a prolonged meeting.

During the playback interview, I asked the Interpreter about his decisions when overlapping talk occurs. First, he mentioned that if the two primary speakers begin at the same time, he interprets what he hears, literally. He said, "I think I am more inclined to go with the voice than I am with signs, I have to be honest. So if they both start at once, I will start signing [interpret what I hear in English]. The Deaf person stops and I continue." When asked if there could be any other reason other than hearing English, he replied, "Is it a matter of equality? This is her office, her territory. So he [the Student] is the outsider coming in so I think that takes a lot of rein, too."

The Interpreter "knows" many things. He knows that this is the Professor's territory; he knows that her conversational style includes persistence on topics; he knows that teachers have more status, if not authority, than students; and he knows that the Student has come to get information from the Professor. As the Interpreter assimilates and acts on these different bits of knowledge, it appears that many of the Interpreter's decisions were acceptable and also appropriate and successful. Decisions that allow the Professor to talk actually favor the Student; it benefits him for the Interpreter to stop him so that the Professor can say what she wants.

Undoubtedly, all these factors and more play a role in interpreter decisions about turns with overlapping talk. To what degree roles, prestige, status, authority, language prestige, culture, and other factors contribute to an interpreter's decisions remains a subject for future study.

Interpreter Turns

One consequence of using an explicit utterance to stop a speaker is that an interpreter takes a turn to do so. Saying "wait-a-minute" (or "hold-your-turn") is not a turn initiated by a primary speaker. In managing discourse flow, interpreters become turn-taking participants to direct and allocate turns to the primary speakers. This is a kind of turn-taking that interpreters do. In this section, however, I describe two other kinds of turns taken by the Interpreter during this meeting. One kind of turn is to offer a turn; both of these are directed at the Student. The second kind of turn is an independent turn in which the Interpreter beckons the Student to say something.

Offering Turns

Offering a turn generally happens when a speaker has made an attempt to say something. In this first example, the Professor has the answering machine on, and the recording is playing. During that talk, the Professor turns and says, "sorry" to the Student and turns back to look at the machine. The Student receives that interpretation, turns to look at the Professor, brings up his hands as if to speak, but changes his mind. In ASL, this can be likened to someone saying, "uhm" and then saying "never mind." As the Student's hands go down, the Interpreter leans forward toward the Student, extends an open palm, and raises his eyebrows which in ASL signals a question. Although the Interpreter does not actually execute any sign (a grammatical unit), his gesture means, "Do you want to say something?"

25
P: (machine=Wednesday September twenty-third)　　　you should
I: (interpreting machine's recording) (look at P)
S:　　　　　　　(look at P----------------------)　　　(look at I)

26
P: Sorry.　　　　　(look at machine------------------------------)
I: HAVE-TO　　　　　　　SORRY　(look at P, turn to S)
S:　　　　　　　　　　(look at P, bring hands up)

27
P: (machine talking, P looking at machine-----------------------)
I: **gesture: palm up, eyebrows up**) SO LEAVE #MESSAGE
S:　　　　　　　　　Gesture "no" (hands down)

Offering a Turn

When the Interpreter offers the opportunity for the Student to take a turn, the Student refuses, and his hands lower (27). Then the Interpreter returns to interpreting the answering machine so that the Student will know that the machine problem continues. Knowing that one primary participant is preoccupied and that people can work a machine and talk at the same time, it is reasonable to offer the Student an opportunity to say something.

In the next example, again the Interpreter offers a turn to the Student. The Professor has just offered a final solution to the problem of when the Student should turn in his transcript. She has suggested that he make copies to pass out the next week to be included with the copies she will make of transcripts that are turned in today. As this portion winds down, both begin to utter short responses like "ok" and "good." After the Student says "WELL" which could mean he thought of something to say, the Interpreter gestures—a slight lean forward, an open palm extended toward the Student, and eyebrows raised, as if to say "Do you want to say something?"(212).

```
211
P:
I: FOR NEXT-WEEK  PUT-IN-FILE  PASS-OUT  ALL HAVE IT
S:                             OK         GOOD
```

```
212
P:              ok
I: ok   That's good      good    #OK    gesture  GOOD
S:             "WELL"                     FINE (repeated)
```

```
213
P:
I:              ok              Thank you
S: FINE  OK           THANK YOU
```

Again, the Interpreter offers a conversational opening for the Student as if to say "is there anything else you want to say?" Again, the Student does not have a question or a content message so he just says, knowing that this topic is coming to an end, "that's fine."

What is interesting about offering a turn is that the Interpreter must take a turn to offer a turn. Both taking a turn and offering a turn are indicative of the complex nature of an interpreter's involvement in the

communicative process of an interpreted event. The Interpreter's participation in the flow of discourse supports the findings of Berk-Seligson
(1990), Metzger (1995), Wadensjo (1992, 1998), and others, suggesting
that the nature of an interpreter's rights and obligations bear intensive,
continued study. When, in other situations, do interpreters offer turns?
And, how do interpreters know when to offer turns?

Taking a Turn

This segment is, perhaps, the most significant extract of talk from the
entire meeting. Within this span, the Interpreter intervenes to beckon the
Student to say something. This activity in the discourse process marks
the potential breadth and scope of an interpreter's ability to influence
both the direction and outcome of this event. These decisions, more than
any other, are indications of experience and the accumulated knowledge
of how these social scenes should play out so that all participants experience an outcome that is satisfactory.

This segment becomes a negotiation between Professor and Student. As the discussion of linguistic features in the transcript comes to an
end, the Student asks if he should revise the transcript for next week's
class. The Professor wanted it today (Wednesday) but asks the Student if
he could have it ready the following Monday. The Student told the Professor previously that he would be out of town for the weekend giving a
presentation, implying that he cannot have it ready for Monday. The
Student repeats this information, and the conversation comes to a halt. At
this point, the Interpreter leans forward and executes a beckoning gesture
to the Student. The Interpreter urges the Student to say something.

175
P: Well could it be possible at all to get it to me by Monday?
I: SAY   POSSIBLE
S:

176
P:
I: IF CAN GIVE-ME MONDAY? CAN GIVE-ME ON MONDAY? ASK?
S:

177
P:
I: hum   Monday (soft laugh)
S: MONDAY

178
P:
I: uh because I get back   from Rochester Sunday
S: COME-BACK FROM ROCHESTER SUNDAY

179
P: ok uhm (looks at floor------------------------------------)
I: uh   **gesture** (hands open, body forward, direct gaze)
S:

180
P:
I: How 'bout   Wednesday morning?
S: WEDNESDAY   MORNING

189
P:
I: Before class?
S: BEFORE CLASS?

"Say something"

When the Professor asks if the Student could give her the transcript by Monday, the Student says, "I get back from Rochester Sunday" and stops talking. The Professor says 'ok' and 'uhm' and looks at the floor (179). The Interpreter already knows that the Student has said the wrong thing because the Interpreter's 'uh' as the Professor says 'ok' is not a rendering of anyone's talk, and he opens the possibility that there is more to be said. And, in fact, the Interpreter does *not* interpret what the Professor says, rather he leans forward and with a gesture bids the Student to talk (179). Right on cue, the Student does; he offers a solution: "How 'bout Wednesday morning? Before class?

The Interpreter, recognizing that, typically, American students do not tell professors "no" either directly or indirectly when asked to turn in an assignment, prompts the Student to say more. In so doing, the Interpreter takes a self-motivated turn and influences the outcome of this interaction.

Practicing interpreters might suggest that this action by the Interpreter violates professional codes of conduct—those concerned with interfering in a situation. But I would argue that the Interpreter has instead followed the first "commandment" of any interpreting code of conduct—to interpret the "spirit and intent" of a message. The Interpreter, knowing that the Student may not know or may not always be able to apply appropriate ways of speaking in these situations, has assisted the Student in behaving appropriately during this interaction.

The Student spent all his academic years, up until now, in educational institutions geared toward Deaf persons, a state school for the Deaf and Gallaudet University, the only liberal arts university for the Deaf in the world. Although everyone he has encountered may not have known how to use ASL, they've accommodated Deaf "ways of speaking" or have presented skewed versions of ways of speaking and behaving in traditional American institutions. As sociolinguists have argued, many ethnicities in the United States maintain their own "ways of speaking" and do not flourish in American mainstream situations.

That interpreters offer turns and even take turns of their own alters the direction and perhaps even the outcome of interpreted conversational exchanges. The nature of this activity has only recently begun to be studied and, obviously, demands further study.

Managing Communication

The turn exchange system of interpreting mirrors the possibilities of ordinary turn exchanges in any language. Smooth transitions, potential gaps or pauses, and overlapping talk are all features of turn-taking processes in any language. However, in face-to-face encounters which are interpreted, interpreters actively involve themselves in the ebb and flow of talk.

Interpreters are an integral part of the exchange process. Speakers cannot know possible transition moments in other languages, nor can they know what pauses are or how turns end. They participate only in their own language. Thus, two turn-taking systems are operating independently of each other while yet another system, a discourse exchange system, is controlled by an interpreter.

All primary participants within any discourse event interact in complex ways. Together, speakers and interpreters create pauses, overlapping talk, and turns. Although speakers attend to the interaction because of the reasons that brought them together, interpreters attend to interaction management and make decisions about the discourse process itself. Interpreters are doing more than searching a lexical bank, or syntactic rules, to create coherent utterances and turns. They act on understandings and expectations of the way social scenes emerge in interaction, as well as on social and cultural knowledge of the "ways of speaking" within particular situations. Choosing appropriate equivalents depends more on the relative status of the interlocutors and desired outcomes than on grammatical or semantic factors.

Some scholars might suggest that the complexity and uniqueness of this event lies solely in the fact that one participant is using a linguistic system of a different modality (ASL). However, I argue that the mode of a linguistic system has very little to do with the nature of interpreting as a face-to-face interaction. Pauses, simultaneous talk, and confusion regarding turns exist during interpreting no matter which linguistic system is in use. A speaker who knows only German cannot know the import or intention of a response from a speaker who knows only Yoruba (a language of Nigeria) any better just because the languages are spoken and not signed.

Interpreters are members of interpreted conversations, involved in creating turn exchanges through their knowledge of the linguistic system, conventions for language use, the social situation, and the discourse structure system. Experienced interpreters, then, are competent bilinguals (or multilinguals) who possess knowledge of two (or more) languages and also knowledge of social situations, "ways of speaking," and strategies for managing communication. Finally, the interpreter is not solely responsible for either the success of the failure of interpreted interaction. All three participants jointly produce this event, and all three are responsible, in differing degrees, for its communicative success or failure.

Accounting for and determining the role of different rights and obligations of speakers and how this knowledge influences interpretations is an ongoing discussion that the profession must have. Although interpreters may know and act instinctively on this knowledge, it is my experience that neither practitioners nor students study, practice, talk about, or reflect on decisions about discourse processes, such as turns and overlapping talk. What is missed in not acknowledging or studying this level of knowledge is that experienced interpreters intuitively and successfully interpret the pragmatic meanings of discourse events more often than not, and, subsequently, these situations turn out much as they would if the two primary speakers did speak a common language. Although these individual events may turn out successfully, without further research and study, there is not pattern or consensus for teaching interpreting to entering students, for teaching successful strategies, or for competently certifying interpreters.

8

Role Performance in an Interpreted Discourse Process

Conduit Metaphors

From the previous chapter it is clear that an interpreter's role is more than that of passing messages back and forth; it is also a role that manages the communication process of exchanging those messages. In this chapter, I begin with a discussion of how the role has been and, in many ways, still is conceived. To investigate further the performance of that role and its implications for norms in interpreting, I analyze four examples of interpreter performance.

Practicing interpreters are aware of the public and professional expectations of and demands on their practice, most of which are concerned with confidentiality, neutrality, accuracy, and faithfulness to the message. Interpreters often describe their role "as the person in the middle" by using a metaphor which conveys the image or impression that they serve as a bridge or channel through which communication happens. This channel is supposed to relay a message from one speaker to another faithfully, accurately, and without personal or emotional bias. The performance of this role has been compared to a machine, a window, a bridge, and a telephone line—among others—when trying to compress the complexity of the role into a simple, singular analogy or metaphor.

This perspective developed, in part, from practitioners, educators, and researchers who have devoted the bulk of their attention to interpreters working within public and monologic contexts. In these public forums interpreters usually are interpreting for speakers who speak one at a time to typically nonresponsive audiences. In these events, an interpreter's role appears conduit like, passive, and noninvolved.

Another reason for the persistence of this perspective lies in past research on interpreting which has been done largely by cognitive psychologists and psycholinguists who have focused on the phenomena of language processing and transference of information. This research on the complexity of listening, understanding, and speaking simultaneously has produced detailed models of the psycholinguistic stages of transfer based on errors revealed in the target language production (Cokely 1984; Moser-Mercer 1978). Although these models provide better understanding and appreciation of the mental complexity of interpreting, their very nature reinforces the metaphorical image through which interpreting is perceived. Unfortunately, the force of this perspective is such that most training and professional testing still (in 1998) devote their efforts to the details of the interpreted message and its form.

Although the conduit metaphors developed partially in response to a particular situational performance and to the direction of research studies, they are also used because of ordinary perceptions about the nature of language and communication. Lakoff and Johnson (1980) found that although most people think of metaphors as devices of poets and rhetorical style, they are prevalent in our everyday lives because they allow us to present our conceptual systems through language. Metaphors structure how we think about and preceive our everyday lives. Reddy (1979) explains how ordinary language use portrays language as a conduit which passes on a speaker's thoughts and ideas to a listener whose only task is to unwrap the thoughts and ideas that have been transmitted through a conduit and thus hides aspects of the communication experience.

The words we use to talk about how ideas are shared are indicative of a conduit notion. For example, "I *gave* you that idea." It seems hard to see a metaphor here at all. The word 'give' seems ordinary enough until we ask ourselves if ideas have a concrete substance that can be given to someone else. These ordinary metaphors convey the sense that meaning actually resides in words, phrases, and sentences as a tangible object to be inserted or taken out.

These metaphors also lead us to particular ways of thinking about the originator of the message, the message itself, and the receiver of the message. For example, "Try to pack more thoughts into fewer words." This type of expression blames the speaker for failing to put enough meaning in or failing to put the meaning in the right place. Equally, in the logic of a conduit metaphor, the receiver must unpack the meaning from the words. "Let me know if you find any good ideas in the talk." It's as though ideas can be inserted into words and sentences.

The conduit metaphor implies a whole framework of basic assumptions about language, such as language functions like a conduit transferring thoughts from one person to another, words accomplish a transfer of ideas by containing the thoughts or feelings in the words and conveying them to others, and people can extract exactly the same idea, thought or feeling by simply receiving the words.

These everyday metaphors mold our perceptions about language and communication. Conduit metaphors that abound in the fields of communication, psychology, language, and information processing have been naturally brought into the field of interpreting. It is easy to see how a communication process involving a supposedly neutral or passive third party accepts a conduit-type metaphor as a way of defining itself.

Although these metaphors clearly respond to a need, they also carry double messages. Certainly they convey the idea of transferring messages, but, at the same time, they call to mind images of disengagement and noninvolvement on any other level. Frequently, interpreters are called on by those who use their services to be "flexible" and in fact are called upon by their own colleagues to be so. Standards of ethical practice extensively, sometimes exhaustively, list what interpreters should *not* do, but they seldom explain what interpreters can, or should do, or where or how flexibility should be exercised. Consequently, discussions of practice fall back on what interpreters should not do, or what interpreters *may* do within the guidelines and wind up being discussions of ethics.

In addition to creating metaphors to describe role performance, interpreters (and others) tend to idealize conversational behavior even though their experience with interaction violates both their notions of relaying messages and of the way conversations should occur. In private conversations, interpreters confess to "breaking the rules" while also admitting that their rule-breaking behavior was successful.

What interpreters actually know (intuitively or objectively) and do is complex from both the perspective of psycholinguistic processes and also from the perspective of interactive communication systems as a whole. Interpreters are not simply processing information and passively passing it back and forth. Their task requires knowledge of a discourse system that includes grammar, language use, organization, participant relationships, contextual knowledge, and sociocultural knowledge. Interpreters must also have the ability to adapt this knowledge quickly to size up a situation, anticipate problems, and decide on solutions within seconds which means they operate within an emergent system of adaptability.

Because standards of practice have developed before we have described and analyzed what interpreters do as they work, interpreters use the language of ethical behavior to talk about their job performance. One way in which interpreting as a discourse process can work for interpreters is in providing new ways to describe, name, and discuss the interpreting process. As this study and the work of Wadensjö (1992), Metzger (1995), and others has shown, interpreters interact in multiple ways within the communicative event of interpreting.

Role Expectations

As Goffman (1961) suggests, when exploring what a particular role is, one would naturally take a look at the normative expectations associated with the role. These expectations come primarily from interpreters themselves: what they have theorized an interpreter should do as the person-in-the-middle. Typically these expectations have centered on the delivery of messages between speakers, their accuracy and adherence to meaning, and the lack of bias. However, as interpreters themselves have said, what is idealized as correct practice is not what happens in reality. For example, in *Interpreting: An Introduction*, when Frishberg, the author, interviews an interpreter and asks about responsibility in practice, the interpreter suggests that interpreters have to be "communication cops": "And the interpreter needs to take on as part of their role, as "communication cop," because they're the bilingual person in the situation, and they're going to know the timing and the rhythm and the pause sequencing and the languages and know when is an appropriate time" (Frishberg 1986: 28). These remarks echo conversations heard for years among interpreters. During the reality of work, it becomes apparent that interpreters do more than convey messages. What interpreters struggle with is how to explain this activity best and how to decide whether the activity is ethical.

What remains is to describe and examine what interpreters do as they work in interactive events. Because speech events and discourse processes *are* interactive and meanings accumulate through the interaction, an interpreted event cannot be understood by examining only the interpreter. "When studying a social role, the *constellation* of people is the basic analytical unit, *not* the individual" (Wadensjö 1995: 115; emphasis hers). In exploring the role within an interactive framework, an analyst must investigate how roles are actually performed and how others in the activity act and react to confirm or deny the performance of roles. Interpreters act in concert with other participants; their speech and actions cannot be understood adequately or accurately without considering the speech and actions of the other two participants.

Let's begin by examining the flow of talk in an idealized interpreted conversation. Borrowing from Wadensjö (1995: 116), the following is a portrayal of an idealized conversation in which an Interpreter (I) and two primary participants talk. One participant is typically a professional (P), such as a doctor or a lawyer, or a representative of an institution, either private or governmental. The other participant is an ordinary citizen (C) who speaks a minority language.

P:	Utterance 1 (the majority language)
I:	Utterance 1a (rendition of U1)
C:	Utterance 2 (the minority language)
I:	Utterance 2a (rendition of U2)
P:	Utterance 3
I:	Utterance 3a
Etc.	

Following idealized norms, an interpreter is expected to interpret in sequence, one turn after another, and interpret only what primary parties say. Official norms also demand that this middle-person position or role is that of a neutral participant, one who does not take sides, offer opinions, or show bias. This neutrality is reflected in the idealized version of conversational turn-taking in the example. If interpreted conversations proceed according to an idealized version, then, participants exchange turns on an equal basis in an organized manner: speaker A, interpreter, speaker B, interpreter, and so on.

I have already demonstrated that, in fact, interpreted conversations are complex activities and turns are not exchanged on the basis of speaker A, then interpreter, then speaker B because speakers do not always speak on a turn-by-turn basis nor do participants assume equal rights or obligations to speak. In Chapter 7, the analysis revealed that simultaneous talking, for example, and turns taken by the interpreter, suspend idealized versions of talking and turn-taking.

When Primary Participants Talk to Interpreters

To be realistic about an interpreter's role, we can examine several more examples of the way speakers interact and take turns. In this first example, I look at a turn in which a primary participant speaks directly to the Interpreter. Because examples from this case study corpus are relatively limited, I will add another example that appeared in an interpreter membership association newsletter.

Interpreters complain frequently about the propensity of primary participants to address utterances directly to interpreters. They imply that the primary participants should know better; they should know that interpreters only relay messages; they do not answer or speak directly to participants. Interestingly, their complaints seem to focus on the participant who is the professional or institutional representative, generally a speaker of a majority language, not the citizen or client, who speaks a minority language. Asking a question or speaking directly to an interpreter affords an opportunity to study the interaction around this dilemma, to examine different responses, and to learn whether primary participants are confirming or denying the role performance of the interpreter.

In the interpreting event studied in Chapter 7, the Student poses a question directly to the Interpreter. As the three participants sit down and begin to talk, the telephone rings, and the Professor answers it. As she answers the phone, the Student asks the Interpreter if the Researcher is filming.

S: FILMING?   pointing at the researcher FILMING?
I: [to the researcher]   FILMING?   Are you filming?
R: yes
I: YES [to the Student]

The Student wants to know if filming has begun so he poses the question to the Interpreter. The Interpreter then asks the Researcher (who understands ASL) first using ASL, then asking in English. Because the camera lens was fogged and the Researcher could not see clearly (a problem that cleared up), she did not respond to the signed utterance. When she heard the question, she answered in English, and the Interpreter relayed the answer to the Student.

Although the Interpreter does relay this query from the Student, he is *supposed* to relay this question to the Professor as the other *primary* participant. In interpreting ideology, interpreters are not supposed to answer direct questions; rather they should pass on the question to allow the primary speaker to answer (see Metzger 1995: Chap 5). The Researcher is an ancillary participant who is supposed to be ignored because she is filming the event. But the Interpreter did relay the question on to a participant other than himself. That leaves two questions to be asked: To whom was the question directed? Why didn't the Interpreter relay the question to the Professor?

Let us begin with the second question. The Interpreter did not relay the question to the Professor because she was answering the telephone and was speaking to the person who called. In conversational interaction, one primary participant can be called to attend to other matters or conversations, a perfectly ordinary occurrence in interaction. For example, when I accompany my mother to the lawyer's office, the lawyer occasionally interrupts the meeting to answer a phone call or conduct a side conversation with his secretary. While he is engaged, my mother and I talk over what she and her lawyer are discussing, or something else entirely. In this interaction, when the Professor is otherwise engaged, the Student can and does ask the Interpreter a question about the other activity at the meeting. So the Interpreter does not relay the question to the Professor because the question was not directed at her.

Now let's consider the first question: To whom was the question directed? Because the Student could see the Professor using the phone and because he asked the Interpreter, rather than turning around and asking the Researcher, and simply pointed in the direction of the Researcher, the question seems to be directed at the Interpreter. Most likely, the Student thought that the Interpreter could answer because video cameras generally have lights that come on when filming.

My point here is that a primary participant spoke directly to the Interpreter *when* the other primary participant was not attending to the interaction and had "absented" herself from the interaction with the Student. Participants act and react to interpreters as potential conversational partners and seem unaware that the task of interpreting should preclude treating an interpreter as a potential interlocutor. To primary participants, then, it must seem natural, even ordinary, to interact with interpreters as capable human beings who can answer and ask questions. This might suggest to interpreters that primary participants are never going to act as though interpreters are not also real participants in the interaction. It also suggests that interacting directly with an interpreter does not come about arbitrarily, but rather because of other social norms that govern interaction when a primary participant is interrupted and moves the focus off the reason and purpose for coming together.

My next example is drawn from an article in *Views* (January 1998), the newsletter of the Registry of Interpreters for the Deaf, a North American association of sign language interpreters. In this article, the author presented an example similar to the previous one: a primary speaker asks an interpreter a question. The situation was a doctor's office where a Deaf patient was being examined. During the examination the doctor turns to the interpreter and asks, "How did you get into the field? Is sign language hard to learn?" The dilemma presented to readers was that the interpreter was asked a question by the doctor but was not sure how to handle this situation or who should answer the question. The author suggested that determining a solution is a matter of ethics and that knowing ways of solving ethical dilemmas assists interpreters, particularly beginning interpreters, in arriving at good solutions. Although I agree that student interpreters should be trained to solve ethical dilemmas, under the scrutiny of discourse analysis, this particular phenomenon might not be an ethical problem but rather an ordinary happenstance in the interactional process of discourse.

We can begin by noting that no other information is provided about the meeting and its progress. The doctor's question is presented in isolation. As the preceding example demonstrated, it matters what the other participants are doing. We do not know what the patient is doing, what was said prior, or what is said afterward. This is the point about studying interpreters in actual interaction. Utterances do not arise on their own but are created in and reflected by the ongoing situation, and understanding or interpreting utterances is based on and is particular to that context. The patient could be changing clothes, could be having her temperature taken, or could be in the bathroom.

The next thing to consider is that whether or not people are engaged in purposeful activity that may have serious consequences, such as a medical exam, they also monitor relationships, attitudes, and feelings. When doctors examine patients, it is not out of the ordinary to engage in small talk which seems to put everyone at ease. Nor is it unusual, when patients are unavailable for conversation, for doctors to engage in brief conversations with other person(s) in the room. Once, while my teenager was having her temperature taken, a doctor turned and began chatting with me about the extreme heat we were experiencing that summer. In general, all the participants engaged in interaction are available for conversation (Goffman 1967). In some ways, professionals, such as doctors and lawyers, experience a sense of being "hosts" within their spaces and thus attempt to acknowledge all the participants within the space, either by conversation or nonverbally.[1]

As people engage in small talk, however, they do not expect this type of talk to grow out of proportion to its significance. In other words, in serious activities, such as medical exams, questions like, "How did you get into the field?" and How did you learn sign language?" anticipate brief responses. These questions are more about acknowledging presence, establishing contact, and showing interest than about learning information. These questions are participant-oriented, not true queries for information. An extended answer or an answer diverted to another participant would seem unnecessary and disruptive to the flow of conversation.

Because interpreters are human and participate in the discourse process, it seems natural, even ordinary, for speakers, especially those unfamiliar with interpreters, to view them as participants capable of answering questions. Not only is the doctor's question a natural, direct question that one could anticipate from those unfamiliar with Deaf people and their language, but one can also anticipate that the doctor expects a brief answer to be forthcoming from the interpreter with minimal time elapse.

However, as specialists in assisting with communication, interpreters know that these direct questions have the potential of distracting or disrupting the more important conversational flow occurring here. Thus, for interpreters, this is a communicative dilemma, and the central question around interpreter involvement could be how to minimize this conversational participation rather than whether or not the other participant has a right to know and answer the question or direct the interpreter to answer.

Managing conversational flow, so that the speakers accomplish their purposes for meeting, would seem to include keeping distractions to a minimum. The author's options for solving the dilemma were to relay the question to the Deaf patient and either relay an answer back or get the Deaf person's permission to answer. Both of these solutions result in a longer than expected wait for an answer for the doctor. Questions and answers are utterance pairs because questions anticipate and expect answers.[2] Although both options would eventually be a response, these options (1) delay an anticipated quick response and (2) do not answer the question; rather, both responses suggested point out the role and responsibility of the interpreter, a question not even conceived by the doctor.

Metzger (1995) has shown that giving explanations or delaying responses by sending the question onto the other participant causes *more* interruption in a discourse event: "Minimal responses allowed interaction to resume with the *least* amount of influence of the interpreter" (232). Answering briefly minimizes the disruption of the interactional flow or rhythm and is a course of communicative action that contributes to maintaining a flow of talk to achieve the speakers' actual purposes for coming together.

Passing the question along to the minority speaker comes from the notion that interpreters' loyalty should lie with Deaf people. The argument is that to relay the question to the Deaf person grants that person the power to control their own situation. But research suggest that this solution is in fact more disruptive than necessary. Interpreters are, by the very nature of their work, committed to Deaf people or minority citizens and to their right to control their destiny and to be treated as first-class citizens. Moreover, Deaf people and minority citizens who go to doctors have a lot more important things on their minds than whether or not the doctor understands the role of an interpreter.

Let us return to the point of how roles are defined by those who inhabit the role and are also defined by the way the others confirm or reject the performance of the role. Although we do not have the possible or potential reaction of the doctor to a delayed response, we can see that this would indeed confirm or deny how the role plays out in actual interaction. If either participant reacts in a way that presents interactional problems, then one can see their expectations for the role of interpreter. When one of the interpreters in Metzger's study did not answer a direct question and passed the question along to the minority speaker, the interaction became considerably more confused (1995: Chap. 5). Interactional confusion would seem to be what an interpreter should be responsible for fixing, not causing.

Other points can be made here. First, this example should illustrate the potential difficulties of taking utterances out of context. As people talk, meaning is created in and by the relationships established, by previous knowledge and experience in interaction, by words and sentences, and by the way utterances occur sequentially. One of Schiffrin's central principles of discourse is that "how something is said, meant, and done . . . is guided by relationships among the following:

1. Speaker intentions
2. Conventionalized strategies for making intentions recognizable

3. The meanings and functions of linguistic forms within their emerging contexts
4. The sequential context of other utterances
5. Properties of the discourse mode—narrative, description, and exposition
6. The social context-participant identities and relationships, structure of the situation, and the setting
7. A cultural framework of beliefs and actions (1994: 416)

Without considering some or all of these relationships, utterances can be analyzed only in terms of their surface meanings. Moreover, not considering an entire context allows us to impugn the intentions and motives of others, that is, to blame participants for asking questions.

We cannot understand how an interpreter's role emerges in actual interaction by simply hypothesizing what that role should be. The reality of practice does not conform to the ideology. This example does allow us to ask about or ponder the expectations for interpreters to act as full participants and, likewise, to ask about or ponder the obligations of interpreters to respond as participants and to initiate actions through language as full participants. This then is where the boundary of ethical decisions might lie.

Goffman, Participant Alignments, and Role

All of us *perform* (to use Goffman's description of the way we enact different aspects of self) multiple roles, such as woman, mother, professor, and citizen; and as we shift from one role to another, we change the way we talk to others. These changes can also signal changes in meaning: we might say the same word but have very different ideas about what it means—the word 'justice,' for example—as well as changes in other features of language, such as intonation or stress, which signal whether we mean something sarcastically or literally, for example. This framework and its analytical terms have been used extensively by discourse analysts (see Schiffrin 1994; Tannen 1993) and by my colleagues, Wadensjö (1992) and Metzger (1995), to explain the shifts interpreters make from relaying messages to managing or coordinating talk. Here I present another example where a primary participant speaks directly to an interpreter and the interpreter speaks back to this participant. This example, taken from Wadensjö (1995), includes the information we did not have about the previous interaction. Wadensjö, building on the work of Goffman and Gumperz, shows how a primary participant speaks specifically to the interpreter and how the interpreter responds; primarily, Wadensjö argues, because the primary participant shifted the alignment toward the interpreter and treated the interpreter as a speaker who would respond from the stance of a full participant.

Goffman (1976, 1981) has written about the complex ways in which conversational interactants both speak and listen to each other. Goffman (1981) explained that speakers could be talking yet not saying words of their own creation, for example, reciting a poem or translating. Wadensjö (1992) suggested thinking of these differences as displaying aspects of speaking and thus a speaker could be taking or denying responsibility for what is said and meant. Expanding on Goffman's terms for different aspects of speaking or *production formats*, Wadensjö added that when speakers are *animators* of talk, then the authority and responsibility for what is said belongs to someone else. When speakers are *authors* of talk, the person speaking decides what words to use, but the authority or responsibility for what is said belongs to another. As *principals* of talk, a speaker is both animator and author and has both the authority and responsibility for what is said. Wadensjö important contribution is to further Goffman's analysis to include listeners, so that the role of listener is shown to have different aspects of listening, or different *reception formats*: "The idea is that you can determine from the way a person is listening that she takes more or less responsibility for the progression and the substance of common interaction" (Wadensjö 1995: 121-122). Wadensjö proposed matching listener terms of *reporter, recapitulator,* and *responder* to correspond to aspects of speakers outlined by Goffman. Listening to repeat exactly is listening as a *reporter*. Listening to summarize is to listen as a *recapitulator*, and listening to respond adequately is a *responder*. One way of listening does not necessarily exclude another, but the way in which a person responds indicates what kind of listening is predominant or on which aspect the listener is focused.

In discourse, when participants shift into a different alignment, or footing (Goffman's term), their alignment to others changes, and all participants, including the interpreter, shift their inferences about utterances. Thus, if an interpreter, when listening to a primary participant, hears/sees a change in the way a primary participant is talking, then the interpreter may also shift to come into alignment with that participant. In this way, an interpreter's role is subject to shifting influences from both within and without in interaction, just as any speaker is. Wadensjö (1995: 117-120) provides the following example.

A Russian-speaking woman, Alisa, has been called to the immigration department at a Swedish police station. She is interviewed about her application for a residence permit in Sweden. Peter, the official, is to interview her and write a report on the basis of which her case will be decided. The interpreter is Ilona. Peter asks Alisa to speculate, to think about how she can use her profession in Sweden. Alisa replies, "Well . . . I think that. I have to retrain myself." After the interpretation, Alisa goes on to say that she doesn't know Swedish and comments on the level of development of the medical profession in the two countries (Alisa is a midwife/gynaecologist). A few utterances later, Peter returns to the expression "retrain oneself" and asks about the meaning of this expression.

> Peter: Aha. Retrain oneself. Yes yes okay. You-you mean to
> get some knowledge in Swedish. or do a refresher
> course? Or er I have problems with the expression
> retrain oneself. Then I think about an entirely dif
> ferent profession. Can we clear this up, just a little.

> Ilona: a no it-it was my fault. Thi-This was just what she had
> in mind.

First, when Peter asks what Alicia means about retraining, Ilona, the interpreter, apologizes and then provides a clarification of what Alisa meant (albeit the clarification sounds vague). Wadensjö suggests that if we were to apply interpreting ideology, Ilona has violated the code of "just interpret" by answering the official directly, and by doing so, she prevented the two speakers from an exchange to clarify what was meant.

However, if we use Wadensjö's concept of reception formats, interpreters both listen to understand and listen to repeat. Ilona, as are all interpreters, is caught on an utterance by utterance basis because of her first priority, which is to listen to repeat. Returning to the beginning of the segment, when Alisa, the Russian immigrant, first began to speak, she was formulating her thoughts and as she talked, her meaning became clearer and more specific. As she clarified what she was thinking, Ilona's translation for "retrain oneself" no longer fit the type of meaning, toward which Alicia was headed. So when the official asks for clarification, Ilona accepts responsibility for the interpretation, apologizes, and connects the meaning of retrain to Alisa's final remarks about learning Swedish.

Wadensjö suggests that Ilona responds directly to Peter, the Swedish official, because of what Peter says toward the end of his request for clarification, "Can we clear this up, just a little bit." As he finishes, he directs this last remark toward Ilona, as Wadensjö explains: "If the first part of his utterance could well be understood as relating to Ilona as *recipient-reporter* (i.e., Alisa is referred to in his "you mean" etc.), the end of it, in a lower voice, sounds rather as if relating to the interpreter as *responder* or *recapitulator*, i.e., as someone included in his pronoun of address ('can we clear this up') (1995: 125). In other words, even though the first part of his utterance could be thought of as addressing Alisa, by the end of his talk, he is addressing Ilona, the interpreter, directly. Peter's contextualization cues, such as his lowered volume and intonation, along with the pronoun shift from "you" to "we," signal the shift from speaking to the other two participants, as he has been, to speaking directly to the interpreter. His final utterance "just a little" is a reminder to the interpreter that time is limited, and the inference was understood as "make the response quick and short." Because the official has shifted his alignment, a shift identified through lexical, prosodic, and paralinguistic cues, the interpreter responds in kind and not only answers but assumes a sense of personal responsibility for the translated expression. When the interpreter first uttered a translation for the expression "retrain oneself," she was listening to it to translate it, but when the official brought the term up again, the interpreter listens as responder-recapitulator, as someone responsible for responding and/or summarizing what is said. A shift occurred in the alignment of these participants, and as Wadensjö points out, for an interpreter, such shifts may fluctuate throughout an interpreting event.

Engaging in talk means that interlocutors coordinate their speaking and listening for their mutual involvement in the discourse. If the interpreter's task is to interpret *and* to coordinate the work of talk, then fluctuating between these two tasks, Wadensjö maintains, can be conceptualized "as two compatible dynamic aspects of the interpreter's interactivity" (1995: 112). Then the interpreter's role has at least two functions, and it is possible for interpreters to shift what they do and also to shift in accepting and denying responsibility for what is said. Part of the point with Wadensjö's example is that the interpreter, Ilona, did accept responsibility for the translation during the actual meeting. Later, when talking with Wadensjö, she vacillated between feeling guilt for her mistake and noting that her translation *was* an acceptable translation, that it was not she who was vague.

This leads to the question, When interpreters shift to managing the communication, what parts of the process of communication become or are the interpreter's responsibility and what parts are not? This is a question for further study, but the next example might highlight the dilemma of this shift.

Reexamining the Interpreter's Role

The example that follows is another look at the Interpreter's turn from Chapter 7 in which the Interpreter urges the Student to talk. Telling, encouraging, or urging a primary participant to talk can perhaps be debated from two perspectives. From one perspective, one could argue that by encouraging the Student to talk, the Interpreter assisted the Student in acting appropriately in a situation where it was important for the Student to act appropriately because it is ultimately a gatekeeping experience (Erickson and Shultz 1982). The Interpreter did not tell the Student what to say, but only prompted him to say something, thus interpreting the "ways of speaking" and norms within a professor-student interaction at a university and which also assisted in maintaining communication.

From another perspective, one might argue that urging any participant to talk is more responsibility for the direction and outcome of a speech event than an interpreter should assume and that the Student might have learned a valuable lesson about interacting with a professor at a relatively early point in his graduate career. To think about these perspectives, I present the example again, transcribed differently. For this discussion I present their utterances line by line, in sequence, without showing where the interpretation overlaps a speaker's utterance. I remind readers that glosses for ASL signs (all caps) represent only a portion of the meaning and can make the ASL seem simplified. In this example, translations of ASL utterances are in italics.

S: YOU WANT ME   IMPROVE   NEXT WEEK CLASS
(Pointing at the paper intermittently)
Do you want me to improve this for next week's class?

I: So uhm you want this to be ready for next week's class?

P: Well could it be possible at all to get it to me by Monday?

I: SAY POSSIBLE   IF POSSIBLE GIVE-ME MONDAY?
POSSIBLE GIVE-ME ON MONDAY   ASK-QUESTION
[she] says Is it possible, it's possible to hand it in on Monday?
Is it possible to give it to me on Monday? I'm asking you.

S: MONDAY (slowly)
Monday

I: Uhm   Monday (laugh)

S: [I] COME-BACK   ROCHESTER SUNDAY
I get back from Rochester on Sunday

I: Uh because I get back   from Rochester Sunday

P: Ok uhm (gaze lowers)

I: Uhm   **gesture** (beckoning the Student to say something)

S: WEDNESDAY MORNING?   BEFORE CLASS?
How about Wednesday morning?   Before class?

I: How about Wednesday morning before class?

P: What I was thinking was having it all ready for everybody by next
week. But let me see how many other people don't have them ready
and.

I: WHY WAIT-A-MINUTE   ME THINK ABOUT CAN HAVE THAT
EVERYTHING READY NEXT-WEEK   OTHERS REMEMBER
COPY-MANY-TIMES ALL   BUT LET ME SEE MAYBE TODAY
Just a second, I was thinking about having everything ready for next
week, remember? The other students? I would copy all their papers,
too, but let me see about today.

Right before this segment begins, there are a few moments of
silence that contribute to a sense of an end to the previous talk and a
change in the direction. Then the Student asks if the paper or assignment
should be ready or improved for Monday, and the Interpreter translates.

The Professor's reply, "Well could it be possible at all to get it to me by Monday?" is a classic indirect request. "Well" is a discourse marker which according to Schiffrin's analysis occurs when answers diverge from the options offered by a prior question (1987: 102-127); "could it be possible" is a conditional which, on the surface, opens the possibility of doing what follows; "at all" is a phrase that almost negates the conditional possibility just opened, followed by the request. Some of the grammatical items make this utterance seem like the beginning of a negotiation, and this is what makes for cross-cultural difficulties. Although the surface structure may indicate that a negotiation is possible, most American graduate students would interpret this as a request not to be denied. The Professor never expected, as she said in her playback interview, to be told no. She does not expect nor want a negotiation, but she has uttered phrases that, on the surface, suggest the possibility of a negotiation.

The Interpreter is caught. After all, the Student is a graduate student in linguistics and has acquired some level of fluency in English if not through speaking, then through writing and reading, and has had a great deal of exposure to English-speaking signers who are constantly code-switching. Translation theory suggests that when minority speakers are literate in their second language, are somewhat bilingual, and are well-educated, interpreters should maintain more of a literal message and strive to match style and voice (Larson 1984; Nida 1969).[3] So, the Interpreter renders a somewhat literal translation of the original message:

English: Well could it be possible at all to get it to me by
             Monday?

Translation: SAY POSSIBLE IF POSSIBLE GIVE-ME
             MONDAY POSSIBLE GIVE-ME MONDAY
             ASK-QUESTION
             *[she] says Is it possible, it's possible to give me
             by Monday? Is it possible to give me on Mon
             day? I'm asking you.*

The changes he makes in translating from the original, explicitly indicating that these are the Professor's words and repeating both words and clauses, stress the surface message for a reason. First, he indicates that he will be reporting her words "SAY [she says]," an unusual thing to do because it has been assumed all along that he is reporting her words. Wadensjö (1992) found an example of this same strategy in her corpus and suggests that interpreters do this to distance themselves even further from the message and its meaning.

In the second clause, the Interpreter signs ON which, in ASL, has the specific meaning of putting a concrete object on another concrete object, as in laying a book *on* a table. Its use here derives from using ASL signs in ways that correspond to English syntax (Winston 1989)and signifies a type of code-switching, which emphasizes the literalness of the translation. Perhaps it is this literalness that is stressed in an attempt to clue the Student that another meaning is lurking about.

Next, the Interpreter repeats the lexical item POSSIBLE three times, twice within a clause which is itself repeated. The first clause has the grammatical question marked on the face, as ASL ordinarily does. In the second clause, however, the Interpreter continues to use question marking on the face, but also adds a specific sign indicating that a question has been asked. The question is asked three times, another repetition.

The most notable aspect of this translation is the repetition of words and clauses. The Professor does not repeat her utterance, but the Interpreter does with clauses that are parallel in structure. Although studies in ASL are only beginning to study the functions of repetition, repetition in general functions to emphasize, and many languages around the world use repeated parallel structures for emphasis (Johnstone 1994). The repetition and parallel structures, the use of code-switching, the added question marker, and the stress on the way the signs are made all reinforce the emphasis on Monday and the sense that the Interpreter is trying to convey another message.

However, the Student fails to interpret the underlying message for himself. He understood that she wanted the assignment by Monday, but he had already told her of his weekend plans which precluded his having the assignment ready Monday. He did not interpret the indirect message as a request not to be denied. We can speculate that the collegial atmosphere created and encouraged by the Professor might have suggested to the Student a sense of permissiveness that did not exist. We can speculate that as a man, and because of gender differences in women and men's language, the Student heard the indirect message as an option to which he could say yes or no (Tannen 1994). We can speculate that the Interpreter did not appropriately convey signals of authority that were particular to the situation. Whatever the reason, the Student interpreted the Professor's utterances as the first part of a negotiation and responded with his own indirect message by talking about returning on Sunday; in essence he said no to the Professor.

Immediately, the Interpreter knows that this response is not appropriate, and we find evidence for that in his talk and action. First, he says "uhm" at the same time the Professor says, "ok uhm." He does not wait for a response from the Student but instead tries to hold the turn with his utterance. Then he leans forward, intensifies his gaze, and gestures for the Student to say something. The Student responds by suggesting Wednesday morning before class.

Although the gesture has worked to get the Student to speak, it is still the "wrong" answer. The Professor wants the assignment on Monday. Even if a student had an engagement over the weekend and could not have it ready by Monday morning, more appropriate responses might have been something like,

- How late will you be here Monday? I can have it in by Monday after noon.
- How early can I get it to you Tuesday morning?
- An apology. May I have one more day?

Rather, the Student is treating this negotiation somewhat like bargaining at a street market, beginning with the options most favorable to him, not to the Professor. In his playback interview, the Student explained that he understood that she wanted the assignment by Monday, but that he could not do that. He did not want to tell her no directly, an indication of his awareness of the use of indirectness in English, so he repeated what he had said earlier indicating a problem turning in the assignment on Monday. He thought that if there was a problem, the Professor, not he, should decide the solution. He mentioned looking at the Professor, seeing that she had stopped talking, then seeing the Interpreter gesture to him to say something more. So he offered another day. Without responding to the Student's offer to turn in the paper on Wednesday, the Professor herself chose an alternative solution. She decided to wait and see how many other students might not have their transcripts ready, and those who did not, could bring them in to the next class meeting on Wednesday with thirty copies. That solved the problem. Although the discussion of what occurred here could continue, I want to turn to the Interpreter and think about his participation in terms of alignment.

Thinking about aspects of alignment, we can examine the shift the Interpreter makes and the resulting change in alignment. As he hears the Professor's indirect request, he knows from experience that indirectness is difficult to interpret, both in the sense of interpreting the underlying message into another language and in the sense of the listener in

understanding indirectness as a nonnative speaker of English. Both linguistic and paralinguistic elements (the repetition and stress) in his translation are indications of a shift, a change of footing, in his alignment to
the Student. Within the discourse, co-occurring factors of language and
situation, a professor talking to a student, serve to motivate a shift in
footing and into a different aspect of his role. As he listens on an utter-
ance-by-utterance basis, he is simultaneously aware of the range of acceptable possible responses from the Student. Recognizing a potential
for miscommunication, he shifts to participating through what he says,
as well as how he listens. As Wadensjö points out, he is fluctuating not
only between the production and reception formats, but also between
different aspects of listening and speaking. This is what she means when
she says about Ilona and interpreters in general that "A dialogue
interpreter's ability to keep in mind different *production formats* and
different reception formats simultaneously, and still be able to keep
them apart, is probably one of her most essential skills" (Wadensjö 1995:
127).

On the surface it might seem that the difference between
Wadensjö's example and mine is whether the primary participant or the
interpreter initiated a shift in alignment. The point we are both making is
that all of the participants are coordinating their talk with each other,
speaking and acting in response to each other and the progression of talk.
This shift, recognized by the Student and acted upon, demonstrates how
the Student's alignment confirms the Interpreter's role as one who should
do this kind of activity. The Student did not question, hesitate, or deny
what the Interpreter did. As Goffman suggested, the other participants act
or react to confirm or deny the role as performed by the participant. Peter,
the Swedish official, confirmed Ilona's performance as he accepted the
answer and continued the interview. Neither of these participants re-
jected the talk and activity of the interpreters. In both examples, the
colluding participant acted in ways that corroborate the role.

The major difference between Wadensjö's example and the example in this case study is the information that the interpreter has. In the
Swedish-Russian example, the information that clarifies the term has
already been spoken. The interpreter knew the information and was not
guessing what the Russian-speaking woman meant. She simply confirmed
that the most recent direction in the discourse was correct. In the example
from this study, the Interpreter could not know what response the Student
might make, so that all he could do was prompt. The Interpreter knows
that another answer is needed, but he cannot supply it because the Student has not supplied it.

In both discourse events, the interpreters are fixing the way something was said and meant, focusing on aspects of discourse that are connected to relationships, attitudes, and feelings. They are accepting responsibility for the flow and maintenance of communication. As Wadensjö (1995) notes in her discussion, by acting as she did in repairing or mediating the Russian immigrant's statement, the interpreter performed an act of "saving face" (Goffman 1976). Simultaneously, her communication with the official kept communication flowing and progressing. In essence, the Interpreter in this study acts similarly. By heading off an interactional problem, he acts to protect the interlocutors "face" and to keep communication flowing, and not lurching to a stop as it seemed it might do. Remember the Interpreter's comments from Chapter 6 that communication is the primary goal: to have people talk to each other and implying that things should not break down. The Interpreter understands that if the Student continues on his path of negotiation, communication has the potential of breaking down. If he understands his primary goal is to keep communication flowing and perhaps to assist minority speakers in acting appropriately in American discourse events, then his words and actions make sense.

Any theory of interpreting must include describing and accounting for the role of the interpreter. Describing and accounting for the role of an interpreter in a discourse event will necessarily be complex in the light of social, interactional, discourse, and personal dimensions. Within any role, then, individuals have both self-images and images that others have of the person who inhabits a role. A consistent and regular performance is an inherent part of performing a professional role (Goffman 1961). Among other things, this gives professionals the right to claim expert opinions on the norms of conduct. But when those opinions do not account for the actual performance of the role in a discourse process, they are invalid. Although interpreting what is said *is* a primary role of interpreters, it is incumbent on the profession to encourage and promote the academic investigation and study of the role as it is performed in interactive discourse.

9

Epilogue

Interpreting as a Discourse Event

As is evident from the analysis presented, the nature and structure of this discourse event is complex due to the interrelationships among the participants and their aims, their expectations and assumptions, the ways in which meaning emerges, and the way participants represent those meanings in their languages. Studying discourse and its phenomena among and between the participants and the interpreter explicates how the interpreting process works and how the interpreter works within it. This type of study begins to tell us how interpreters know what things mean and what strategies they use to convey meaning.

First, the *basic* and *fundamental* interpreting event occurs when two people who have particular intentions and expectations come together and talk through an interpreter. This is the basic nature of human communication and thus is the basic event of interpreting. It is this event that is primary and from which all other interpreted events are derived. It is the interaction here that is central to the study of interpreting, not the interaction when interpreting for a single speaker. The interaction and the presence of the interpreter define the event.

It is also basic and fundamental to the study of interpreting that all three people are part of the process and part of understanding how the process operates. An interpreted event is an exchange of talk among three people, all of whom actively contribute to the direction and outcome of the event. A central requirement of interpreting studies must be to account for all three people as they interact. As Wadensjö eloquently suggests, this is a communicative *pas de trois* (1998:12).

Studying the discourse process of turn-taking demonstrated that regular turns in interpreting can be a smooth transition from one speaker to the interpreter, to the next speaker, and back to the interpreter. Periods of silence between turns or pauses can be separated into three kinds: a natural kind of silence expected in any discourse situation; pausing created by participants; and silences created by lag that are longer than expected, even in interpreting. Overlap, also an ordinary discourse experience, occurs in interpreted discourse even though there is an expected overlap between one speaker and the interpreter. In interpreted discourse, overlap occurs as both primary speakers talk, perhaps even the interpreter is talking, such that interpreters make decisions about the direction of talk. Thus, although interpreted events resemble ordinary discourse events in some ways, they also have their own unique features.

Finally, the interpreter is an engaged participant within the interaction who has particular rights and responsibilities for the communicative process. Interpreters assume certain responsibilities for communication and allow other responsibilities to fall to the other participants. Being responsible for the access and flow of discourse is what interpreters are doing. And what that responsibility entails should be described by research and defined by the profession, not by those who use the services of an interpreter.

Adopting the perspective of studying interpreting events as they proceed in natural interaction and inquiring how such an event took place is based on the understanding that communication requires a great deal of effort and energy on the part of all the participants, but especially on the part of the interpreter. And studying those events will teach us how interpreters do their jobs.

The Role of the Interpreter

The role of the interpreter is created by and performed within the interaction. Analysis of the videotape and transcript have shown how the Interpreter's discourse decisions and shifting aspects of role both create the role and define the role in terms of the other participants' expectations for the role. An interpreter's competence includes knowledge of two languages, knowledge of social situations, "ways of speaking," and strategies for managing the event. Contrary to interpreting belief systems, interpreters are actively involved in interpreting conventions for language use and in creating turn exchanges through their knowledge of discourse systems and social practices, and the way these systems put that knowledge together to create meaning. The interpreter comes to interpreting situations knowing how situations work in the larger society, how social roles influence what people say and do, and how these systems might come into conflict.

In this study the Interpreter exchanged turns with each speaker, created linguistic forms of turns, created some of the unique features, such as lengthy lag, and resolved turn problems, such as overlap. In particular, the Interpreter recognized overlap quickly and made linguistic choices to stop the overlap. Many of his choices exemplified his understanding and interpretation of the social situation involving a meeting between teacher and student. Most significantly, the Interpreter participated in the discourse by taking turns. Taking turns demonstrates how the role allows flexibility when the possibility for miscommunication exists. Although in this event the Interpreter offered turns only to the Student, it is equally likely that turns could be offered or assigned to either participant in another event that has differing constraints. Only interpreters know how a total scene is unfolding; participants consistently volunteer that the one thing of which they are most unsure is knowing when their turn occurs. Taking turns is at the heart of the discourse process and interpreters both control and must accept some responsiblity for the outcome of this process.

Last, but not least, this study has shown that the interpreter is not solely responsible for the success or the failure of an interpreting event. All three participants jointly produce this event and, as such, all three are responsible for the communicative success or failure.

Now, what remains for us to examine is the notion of interpreter neutrality: "Given that neutrality is a notion concerning relations, the question concerning dialogue interpreters' activities must be: neutral in relation to whom and/or what?" (Wadensjö 1992: 268). As Metzger (1995) asks: "Should interpreters, recognizing that they cannot help but function as a participant within an interpreted encounter, no longer strive to be neutral or impartial or should they recognize the paradox of neutrality and strive to minimize their influence on interactive discourse" (220). Both of these imply the other side of the coin: responsibility. So that the other question to be asked is: In what way is neutrality balanced by responsibility? or What are interpreter responsibilities in the process of communicating?

Implications for Teaching

Quality interpreter education is an interdisciplinary endeavor, centered around the mastery of communication-based knowledge and skills. Interpreting students have to learn, in explicit ways, how people communicate meaning when they talk to each other by knowing how variation works in language. The education of interpreters is still evolving from a field that began as an adjunct to foreign language programs and translation programs, or programs teaching sign language. The curricula of such programs typically developed piecemeal and involved, for the most part, classes in language skill development. Teaching interpreting employed the methodology of successive approximation, according to which students are provided with models of simultaneous interpreting and are expected to produce simultaneous interpreting from the outset of their training. The goal of this sort of training was to gradually improve the degree to which the productions of the student approximate the quality of those of the model. Although successive courses did not appreciably differ in content, they were expected to produce successively closer approximations to the ideal.

A second feature of educational programs was the common assumption that the ideal of interpreting was represented by the conference interpreter whose role performance exemplified the relaying nature of the role in which interpreters have little impact on a communicative event and the focus is on message content. Thus, these programs attended to the details of the surface form of the message rather than to the nature of an interactive, communicative event.

An approach to interpreter education that includes the way interpreters participate in a discourse process needs to include courses in which students become familiar with studies of single language discourse; studies in language analysis at both the structural and functional level; and courses in which the emphasis comes from understanding how people create meaning within their cultural, social, and individual styles and practices. Core courses wherein the practice of interpreting is primary including exercises such as paraphrasing, substituting, and clarifying meaning are stressed, are more meaningful when students understand the various ways in which meanings are interpreted. Other exercises which reformulate and restructure messages within a monolingual context to increase students' mastery of each language, working on the agility and flexibility with which they can derive meaning and restructure meaning.

Cokely (1984) has already discussed the need for courses in consecutive interpreting, a task that reduces the immediate cognitive load of listening, analyzing, and thinking simultaneously. As courses in simultaneous interpreting are introduced, they could be divided along the interactional dimension suggested in Chapter 5; one concerning itself with contexts in which conversational interaction occurs, and the other with contexts in which single speakers occur. Supporting the practical skills of interpreting would be courses in professional ethics, demeanor, and business principles.

Another aspect of education includes teaching interpreters to act like ethnographers, analyzing communicative patterns via participant observation. By participating in a wide range of activities in the life of a group of people, students can come to understand different ways of thinking, believing, and acting. They come to know how particular groups "make sense" of their experience and how that experience is rendered through language. This is how interpreters make predictions and acknowledge assumptions. Programs need to find a way to get recorded interactions with and without interpreters so that students can analyze interaction progressively and developmentally with a mentor before they face real time interaction.

Finally, the way we evaluate interpreters will change as we grow to learn what interpreters actually do in performing their role. Evaluation of managing turns, responding, asking questions, and other strategies of the management role should be an important part of testing interpreters. In practice, there are no absolute criteria for defining "good" interpretations. Different discourse events with different goals and needs and different participants require changing actions on the part of the interpreter. Because interpreting involves variable and indefinite utterances from people, the ability to improvise is also a necessary skill (Wadensjö 1992).

Future Research

Research done in other contexts, such as medical, legal, and social services, will undoubtedly clarify other interaction norms of interpreted events, as well as explain to a greater degree how interpreters know what things mean. Among the issues to be addressed by such research are the following:

1. Given that interpreters are influential in ordering and constraining turn exchanges, what other discourse features do they actively manage?
2. What characteristics of primary participants are significant in determining the interpretation of utterances?
3. In what ways are other discourse situations and events similar or different from the event studied here?

Such research would suggest central principles of interpreting theory and would begin to specify the linguistic, sociocultural, and discourse knowledge that an interpreter must have to make decisions and appropriate interpretations.

Professional organizations and membership associations for interpreters should vigorously promote university programs where such research could begin, including funding research centers, institutes, or studies for individual scholars.

A Final Word about Communication

Remembering Reddy's (1979) work on conduit metaphors in ordinary language, it seems fitting to recreate his framework for reconceiving human communication. Creating a contrast between the conduit metaphor and a different metaphorical concept, Reddy suggests a story in which people are likened to toolmakers confined to individual, slightly different, environments who are unable to communicate or show each other tools they have constructed for survival within each environment. In order to communicate their ideas, they exchange sets of instructions that are passed to others through a device that does not allow talking or even a glimpse of the tool itself. As the story unfolds, person A builds a rake, suitable for cleaning her surroundings of leaves and plants, and then tries to communicate the idea of this new tool to others. Person B, however, finds it difficult to interpret the set of instructions because her environment is slightly more rocky. Moreover, stones are the only material available to construct the rake, rather than the wood A has. Since it never occurred to A that other environments could be different from her own, her instructions are difficult for B to follow. As B tries to construct the tool A has built, she builds a different implement. After revising the instructions and creating a new tool, she sends A a new set of instructions. Now A has a set of instructions that are not the same as the ones she sent, and she struggles to interpret what B is doing and why she is building this different tool. As A thinks, she realizes that B must have a different set of requirements for tools. Now A and B send new instructions back and forth. They have raised themselves to a new level of inference about each other and their environments.

In this framework, human communication requires a great deal of energy compared to the conduit framework which implies that successful communication is effortless. In a conduit framework the tool itself would have been exchanged. When person B received A's tool, she would not have to build anything herself or guess at any of the instructions. In terms of language and communication, conduit metaphors imply that a person sends off the actual construct of an idea where it lands fully formed in the mind and understanding of another person. This is success without effort and considering for a moment the individual and social differences found in human beings, we know this is not the case in an exchange of ideas and information.

We can understand why conduit metaphors have such a powerful grasp on our thought processes. If, within our own universe of face-to-face interaction, our communication is with people who share similar backgrounds, knowledge, life experiences, and communicative styles, then talking is easy and understanding facile. Not until we are faced with drastic differences do we find communication demanding, even uncomfortable.

Both of these metaphoric frameworks offer an explanation of communication, but they lead to very different conclusions about what is natural in the activity of communicating and what is less natural: "In terms of the conduit metaphor, what requires explanation is failure to communicate. Success appears to be automatic. But if we think in terms of the toolmakers' paradigm, our expectation is precisely the opposite. Partial miscommunication or divergence of readings from a single text are not aberrations. They are tendencies inherent in the system, which can only be counteracted by continuous effort and by large amounts of verbal interaction. In this view, things will naturally be scattered, unless we expend the energy to gather them" (Reddy 1979: 295–6).

If communication requires a great deal of effort on the part of participants, then interpreting such communication requires even more effort and energy. Reddy's words caution us that rather than explaining failure, or errors in interpreting, we should be asking about the larger system of communicating across languages. Successful interpreting is not effortless and is not automatic. It deserves our attention.

Notes

Chapter 1

1. It is an ordinary expectation that the two primary speakers in an interpreted event do not speak each other's language. It happens occasionally, however, that one speaker does know the other language but perhaps does not speak it well enough, or comprehend it well enough to ensure communication, and thus an interpreter is present (cf Wadensjö 1998).

Chapter 2

1. I include signed languages in the concept of spoken language for this particular discussion because I am distinguishing here between *talk*, whether spoken or signed, and *text*. The transcription of signed languages has been an equally difficult task for reasons described in this discussion and more.

2. Many interactional sociolinguists rely on a more precise transcription of linguistic, including prosodic detail. The example, as presented here, was done so by Gumperz for ease of reading.

3. Conversational analysis followed on the heels of Chomsky and traditions of generative grammar and their search for rule-governed behavior and universal principles unfettered by actual human performance. Generativists were looking for rule-governed behavior at the sentence level; Sacks and his colleagues were looking for rule-governed behavior at the conversational level.

Chapter 5

1. I thank Cecilia Wadensjö for pointing this out to me. As usual her comments have made this a better text.

2. I was also an interpreter and faculty member in the linguistics and interpreting department at Gallaudet University, Washington, D.C. The professor, Dr. Deborah Tannen, is introduced in greater detail in the next chapter.

3. To capture their impressions accurately and to keep conversation flowing, I recorded the professor and interpreter on audiotape and videotaped my interview with the student.

Chapter 6

1. Sign Language interpreters typically sit next to the person who speaks English so that Deaf persons can watch the interpreter while occasionally glancing at the person who is speaking. In addition, it keeps the two primary speakers facing each other as much as possible.

2. It has been my experience and the experience of other interpreters that, even in spoken language interpreting, the primary participants will turn to look at the interpreter even while the other participant is speaking. They seem to be either waiting for the interpretation or paying greater attention to the speaker they can understand.

3. The Student and I were faculty colleagues in the linguistics and interpreting department at Gallaudet University in Washington, D.C. We both taught in the master's degree program for ASL/English Interpreting.

4. The Commission on the Education of the Deaf in 1987 concluded that deaf education in the United States has failed to live up to the expectations and investments of the institutions charged with the instruction of deaf children. Deaf students graduate from high school, on average, reading on the fourth grade level. Gallaudet University, the only liberal arts university for the deaf in the world, revealed in a 1988 survey of entering freshmen that the highest level of academic achievement among deaf students was depressed compared with that of students with average hearing (Johnson, Liddell, and Erting 1989).

5. The Deaf Student's interview was conducted in ASL. The interview was translated by the author and approved by the Student.

Chapter 7

1. American Sign Language is a language in which most of the morphological units are produced with the hands whereas many grammatical elements are produced on the face, in areas of the space in front of the body, and with movements. If represented completely on a transcript, these features would result in difficulty in reading a transcript. Thus the transcript is written to show mostly the main lexical and phrasal units with some grammatical signals represented by marks such as ?.

Because ASL has no orthographic system, this transcript is only for analysis and is only a representation of literal ASL units in English, not a true picture of the entire linguistic system. So the transcript representations for ASL read oddly. For example, if I represented the literal meanings of Spanish in English, it would read something like this:

	Cuantos	años	tienen?
	How-many	years	have-you?
Translation:	How old are you?		

2. Transcript conventions (Tannen 1984, 1989):

.	indicates sentence final falling intonation
,	indicates clause-final intonation ("more to come")
?	indicates yes/no question rising intonation
CAPS	indicates gloss for ASL sign
#	indicates fingerspelling (the representation of alphabetic letters)
+	indicates repetition
hdnd	indicates up-down head motion
PRO1	indicates first person pronoun
PRO3	indicates third person pronoun (singular or plural)

⌐Brackets (with or without top flap) show overlap
└Two voices going at once.   Simultaneously.

Brackets with top flap reversed show latching. ⌐
                                              └No
perceptible inter turn pause.

3. *Latching* is a term that describes when one utterance ends and another begins from another speaker without a perceptible pause.
    4. The Student videotaped a narrative in ASL and planned to show the videotaped ASL version to the class.
    5. It has been suggested to me that overlapping talk of primary speakers would not happen in spoken language interpreting because of its consecutive nature. Empirical studies, however, have shown that overlap of various kinds do indeed occur in spoken language, interpreter-mediated encounters (Dimitrova 1995; Fowler 1995; Wadensjo 1992, 1998). However, I've had many conversations with spoken language interpreters doing community (legal,

educational, social service, medical, etc.) interpreting, who claim otherwise. They tell me that often they begin to interpret before one speaker is finished. They also confide that many times they do so to stop the other speaker. These interpreters have told me that although sequential interpreting is preferable, the structure of modern life forces them toward simultaneous interpreting. Overlap happens, they tell me, when two speakers talk at the same time, or, as I will demonstrate later in the chapter, when two speakers and the interpreter talk at the same time.

6. Two colleagues who are also interpreters and academic researchers, Katherine Langan, Ph.D. (Spanish-English) and Cecilia Wadensjo, Ph.D. (Swedish-Russian) (personal communication), tell me that, in many face-to-face interpreted events, spoken language interpreters are producing overlapping interpretation even when both speakers can hear each other. They also agreed that it's possible for both primary speakers to talk at the same time or begin to talk at the same time which empirical studies of interpreter-mediated encounters have shown (see note 5).

7. This gesture, "wait-a-minute," is a powerful strategy used by interpreters for directing the flow of talk. To demonstrate how powerful this "hold your turn" signal is, thirty seconds later when the Student is talking, the Interpreter reaches out toward the Student with an open palm, not the right index finger. This palm gesture means "hold a second and let me catch up." This time the Student pauses by allowing his hands to remain in midair, and he resumes signing (talking) when the palm is withdrawn.

Chapter 8

1. I am grateful to Katherine Langan for this observation and for her readings and discussions of this chapter.

2. Acknowledging that there are times when answers are not forthcoming.

3. Again I thank Katherine Langan for this point and citations.

Bibliography

Anderson, B. 1976. Perspectives on the role of an interpreter. In R. Brislin (ed.), *Translation: Applications and Research*. New York: Gardner, 208–225.

Anderson, B 1978. Interpreter roles and interpretation situations. In D. Gerver and H.W. Sinaiko (eds.), *Language Interpretation and Communication*. New York: Plenum, 217–230.

Baker, C. 1977. Regulators and turn-taking in American Sign Language discourse. In L. A. Friedman (ed.), *On the Other Hand: New perspectives on American Sign Language*. New York: Academic, 215–236.

Benmaman, V. 1997. Legal interpreting by any other name is still legal interpreting. In S. Carr et al. (eds.), *The Critical Link: Interpreters in the Community*, papers from the first International Conference on Interpreting in Legal, Health, and Social Service Settings, 1995. Amsterdam/Philadelphia: Benjamins, 179–190.

Bennett, A. 1981. Interruptions and the interpretation of conversation. *Discourse Processes* 4(2): 171–188.

Berk-Seligson, S. 1990. *The Bilingual Courtroom*. Chicago: University of Chicago Press.

Brislin, R. (ed.). 1976. *Translation: Applications and Research*. New York: Gardner.

Brown, G., and G.Yule. 1983. *Discourse Analysis*. Cambridge: Cambridge University Press.

Chafe, W. 1980. The deployment of consciousness in the production of a narrative. In W. Chafe (ed.), *The Pear Stories: Cognitive, Cultural and Linguistic Aspects of Narrative Production*. Norwood, N.J.: Ablex, 9–50.

Chafe, W. 1992. Prosodic and functional units of language. In J. Edwards and M. Lampert (eds.), *Talking Data: Transcription and Coding in Discourse Research.* Hillsdale, N.J.: Lawrence Erlbaum Associates.

Cokely, D. 1984. Towards a sociolinguistic model of the interpreting process: ASL and English. Ph.D. diss., Georgetown University, Washington, D.C.

Collard-Abbas, L. 1989. Training the trainers of community interpreters. In C. Picken (ed.), *ITICO Conference Proceedings.* London: ASLIB, 81–85.

Craig, R., and K. Tracy. 1983. *Conversational Coherence: Form, Structure, and Strategy.* Beverly Hills: Sage.

Dimitrova, B. 1997. Degree of interpreter responsibility in the interaction process in community interpreting. In S. Carr et al. (eds.), *The Critical Link: Interpreters in the Community.* Amsterdam/Philadelphia: Benjamins, 147–164.

Duncan, S. 1974. On the structure of speaker-auditor interaction during speaking turns. *Language in Society* 2: 161-180.

Edelsky, C. 1981. Who's got the floor? *Language and Society* 10: 383–421.

Edmundson, W.J. 1986. Cognition, Conversing and Interpreting. In House & S. Blum-Kulka (eds.), *Interlingual and Intercultural Communication.* Tübingen: Gunter Narr, 129–38.

Erickson, F. 1986. Listening and speaking. In D. Tannen and J. Alatis (eds.), *GURT 1985: The Interdependence of Theory, Data, and Application.* Washington, D.C.: Georgetown University Press, 294–319.

Erickson, F., and J. Shultz. 1982. *The Counselor as Gatekeeper: Social Interaction in Interviews.* New York: Academic.

Erting, C. 1982. Deafness, communication, and social identity: an anthropological analysis of interaction among parents, teachers, and deaf children in a preschool. Ph.D. diss., American University, Washington, D.C.

Ervin-Tripp, S. 1969. Sociolinguistics. In L. Berkowitz (ed.), *Advances in experimental social psychology.* NY: Academic Press, 91-165.

Fasold, R. 1990. *The Sociolinguistics of Language.* Oxford: Blackwell.

Fenton, S. 1997. The role of the interpreter in the adversarial courtroom. In S. Carr et al. (eds.), *The Critical Link: Interpreters in the Community.* Amsterdam/Philadelphia: Benjamins, 29–34.

Fowler, Y. 1997. The courtroom interpreter: paragon and intruder. In S.Carr et al. (eds.), *The Critical Link: Interpreters in the Community.* Amsterdam/Philadelphia: Benjamins, 191–200.

Frishberg, N. 1986. *Interpreting: An Introduction.* Silver Spring, Md.: Registry of Interpreters for the Deaf.

Gentile, A. 1997. Community interpreting or not? Practices, standards, and accreditation. In S. Carr et al. (eds.), *The Critical Link: Interpreters in the Community*. Amsterdam/Philadelphia: Benjamins, 109–118.

Gerver, D. 1974. Simultaneous listening and speaking and retention of prose. *Quarterly Journal of Experimental Psychology* 26: 337–342.

Gerver, D. 1976. Empirical studies of simultaneous interpretation: a review and a model. In R. Brislin (ed.), *Translation: Applications and Research*. New York: Gardner.

Goffman, E. 1961. *Encounters: Two Studies in the Sociology of Interaction*. Indianapolis/New York: Bobbs-Merrill.

Goffman, E. 1967. *Interaction Ritual*. New York: Anchor Books.

Goffman, E. 1981. *Forms of Talk*. Philadelphia: University of Pennsylvania Press.

Goodwin, C. 1981. *Conversational Organization: Interaction between Speakers and Hearers*. New York: Academic.

Grosjean, F. 1982. *Life with Two Languages: An Introduction to Bilingualism*. Cambridge, Mass.: Harvard University Press.

Gumperz, J. 1977. Sociocultural knowledge in conversational inference. In M. Saville-Troike (ed.), *28th Annual Round Table Monograph Series on Language and Linguistics*. Washington, D.C.: Georgetown University Press, 191–211.

Gumperz, J. 1982. *Discourse Strategies*. Cambridge: Cambridge University Press.

Gumperz, J., and D. Hymes (eds.) 1972. Preface. *Directions in Sociolinguistics: The Ethnography of Communication*. New York: Holt, Reinhart & Winston.

Harris, Z. 1952. Discourse analysis. *Language* 28:1–30.

Hatim, B., and I. Mason. 1990. *Discourse and the Translator*. London: Longman.

Hoza, J. 1998. The Loyalty Question. *Views* (Newsletter of the Registry of Interpreters for the Deaf), 15 (1): 6–7.

Hymes, D. 1972. Models of interaction and social life. In J. Gumperz and D. Hymes (eds.), *Directions in Sociolinguistics: The Ethnography of Communication*. New York: Holt, Rinehart & Winston, 35–71.

Ingram, R. 1974. A communication model of the interpreting process. *Journal of the Rehabilitation of the Deaf*, 7(3): 3–9.

Ingram, R. 1985. Simultaneous interpretation of sign languages: Semiotic and psycholinguistic perspectives. *Multilingua* 4: 91–102.

Jakobson, R. 1959. On linguistic aspects of translation. In R. Brower (ed.), *On Translation*. Cambridge: Cambridge University Press, 232–239.

James, D. and J. Drakich (eds.). 1993. Understanding gender differences in amount of talk. In D. Tannen (ed.), *Conversational Interaction and Gender*. New York: Oxford University Press, 275–314.

Johnson, R., S. Liddell, and C. Erting. 1989. Unlocking the curriculum: Principles for achieving access in deaf education. Gallaudet Research Institute Working Paper, 89–3. Gallaudet University, Washington, D.C.

Johnstone, B. (ed.).1994. *Repetition in Discourse*. Vol. 1: *Interdisciplinary Perspectives*. Norwood, N.J.: Ablex.

Kochman, T. 1981. *Black and White Styles in Conflict*. Chicago: University of Chicago Press.

Labov, W. 1972. *Sociolinguistic Patterns*. Philadelphia: University of Pennsylvania Press.

Lakoff, G. and M. Johnson. 1980. *Metaphors We Live By*. Chicago: University of Chicago Press.

Lambert, S. 1984. An introduction to consecutive interpreting. In M. McIntire (ed.), *New Dialogues in Interpreter Education*, proceedings of the Fourth National Conference of Interpreter Trainers Convention. Silver Spring, Md.: RID Publications, 76–98.

Lane, H. 1984. *When the Mind Hears: A History of the Deaf*. New York: Random House.

Larson, M. 1984. *Meaning-Based Translation: A Guide to Cross-Language Equivalence*. Lanham, Md.: University Press of America.

McDermott, R., and H. Tylbor. 1983. On the necessity of collusion in conversation. *Text* 3(31): 277–297.

Metzger, M. 1995. The paradox of neutrality: A comparison of interpreters' goals with the realities of interactive discourse. Ph.D. diss., Georgetown University, Washington, D.C.

Metzger, M. 1999. *Sign Language Interpreting: Deconstructing the Myth of Neutrality*. Washington, D.C.: Gallaudet University Press.

Moser-Mercer, B. 1978. Simultaneous interpretation: a Hypothetical model and its practical application. In D. Gerver and H.W. Sinaiko (eds.), *Language Interpretation and Communication*. New York: Plenum, 353–368.

Murray, S. 1985. Toward a model of members' methods for recognizing interruptions. *Language in Society* 13: 31–41.

Nida, E. 1964. *Toward a Science of Translating*. Leiden, the Netherlands: Brill.

Nida, E., and C. Taber. 1969. *The Theory and Practice of Translation*. Leiden, the Netherlands: Brill.

Nida, E. 1976. A framework for the analysis and evaluation of theories of translation. In R. Brislin (ed.), *Translation: Applications and Research.* New York: Gardner, 47–91.

O'Connell, D.C., S. Kowal, and E. Kaltenbacher. 1990. Turn-taking: A critical analysis of the research tradition. *Journal of Psycholinguistic Research,* 19 (6): 345–373.

Phillips, S. 1974. Warm Springs "Indian time": How the regulation of participation affects the progression of events. In R. Bauman and J. Sherzer (eds.), *Explorations in the Ethnography of Speaking.* Cambridge: Cambridge University Press, 92–109.

Potter J., and M. Weatherell. 1978. *Discourse and Social Psychology: Beyond Attitudes and Behavior.* London: Sage.

Reddy, M. 1979. The conduit metaphor: A case of frame conflict in our language about language. In A. Ortony (ed.), *Metaphor and Thought.* Cambridge: Cambridge University Press, 284–324.

Reichman, R. 1985. *How to Get Computers to Talk Like You and Me.* Cambridge, Mass.: MIT Press.

Roberts, R. 1997. Community interpreting today and tomorrow. In S. Carr et al. (eds.), *The Critical Link: Interpreters in the Community.* Amsterdam/Philadelphia: Benjamins, 7–28.

Roy, C. 1989a. A sociolinguistic analysis of the interpreter's role in the turn exchanges of an interpreted event. Ph.D. diss., Georgetown University, Washington, D.C.

Roy, C. 1989b. Discourse features of a lecture in American Sign Language. In C. Lucas (ed.), *The Sociolinguistics of the Deaf Community,* Vol. 1. New York: Academic, 231–252.

Roy, C. 1993. The problem with definitions, descriptions, and the role metaphor of interpreters. *Journal of Interpretation,* 6: 127–153.

Sacks, H., E. Schegloff, and G. Jefferson. 1974. A simplest systematics for the organization of turn-taking in conversation. *Language* 50 (4): 696–735.

Seleskovitch, D. 1978. *Interpreting for International Conferences: Problems of Language and Communication.* Washington, D.C.: Pen and Booth.

Schiffrin, D. 1987. *Discourse Markers.* Cambridge: Cambridge University Press.

Schiffrin, D. 1994. *Approaches to Discourse.* Cambridge, Mass.: Blackwell.

Scollon, R. and S.B.K. Scollon. 1981. *Narrative, Literacy and Face in Interethnic Communication.* Norwood, N.J.: Ablex.

Shuy, R. 1987. A sociolinguistic view of interpreter education. In M. McIntire (ed.), *New Dimensions in Interpreter Education: Curriculum and*

Instruction. Silver Spring, Md.: RID, 1–8.

Shuy, R. 1990. A brief history of American sociolinguistics 1949–1989. *Historiographia Linguistica,* 17 (1–2): 183–209.

Stubbs, M. 1983. *Discourse Analysis: The Sociolinguistic Analysis of Natural Language.* Chicago: University of Chicago Press.

Tannen, D. 1984. *Conversational Style: Analyzing Talk among Friends.* Norwood, N.J.: Ablex.

Tannen, D. 1989. *Talking Voices: Repetition, Dialogue, and Imagery in Conversational Discourse* (Studies in Interactional Sociolinguistics 6). New York: Cambridge University Press.

Tannen, D. (ed.). 1993. *Framing in Discourse.* New York: Oxford University Press.

Tannen, D. 1994. *Gender and Discourse.* New York: Oxford University Press.

Tannen, D. 1994. *Talking From 9 to 5. Women and Men in the Workplace: Language, Sex and Power.* New York: Avon.

van Dijk, T. 1985. Introduction: Discourse as a new cross discipline. In T. van Dijk (ed.), *Handbook of Discourse Analysis.* Vol. 1: *Disciplines of Discourse.* New York: Academic, 1–10.

van Dijk, T. 1997a. *Discourse as Structure and Process.* Vol. 1 of *Discourse Studies: A Multidisciplinary Introduction.* London: Sage.

van Dijk, T. 1997b. *Discourse as Social Interaction.* Vol. 2 of *Discourse Studies: A Multidisciplinary Introduction.* London: Sage.

Wadensjö, C. 1992. Interpreting as interaction: On dialogue-interpreting in Immigration Hearings and Medical Encounters. Ph.D. diss., Linköping University, Linköping, Sweden.

Wadensjö, C. 1995. Dialogue interpreting and the distribution of responsibility. *Hermes, Journal of Linguistics,* 14: 111–129.

Wadensjö, C. 1998. *Interpreting as Interaction.* New York: Longman.

Winston, E. 1989. Transliteration: What's the message? In C. Lucas (ed.), *The Sociolinguistics of the Deaf Community,* Vol. 1. New York: Academic Press, 147–164.

Index

accountability in analysis 51
American Sign Language 49
Anderson, B. 24, 24–25, 28, 61

Baker, C. 88
Bakhtin, M. 30
Benmaman, V. 43
Bennett, A. 37, 37–38, 73, 83
Berk-Seligson, S. 29, 32, 33, 96
Brislin, R. 23, 24, 72
Brown, G. and G. Yule 10

Chafe, W. 10, 71, 81
chunking speech 10–11
Cokely, D. 25, 26, 102, 126
Collard-Abbas, L. 42
communicative competence 20, 24,
    41–43
community interpreting 32–33, 42–43
conduit metaphors 101–104
contextualization cues 13–14, 13–16,
    69–71, 88
conversation analysis 18–19
conversation management 19
conversational data 4–5, 6–7
coordinating interaction 30–32, 32–33
Craig, R. and K. Tracy 9

creating turns 37
Critical Link 32

decision making process 27, 87–93
Dimitrova, B. 32
discourse
    analyzing discourse 4–6, 50–51
    as communication 128
    as language use 10–11
    as lecture 44–45
    as process 10, 21–22
    as structure 10
    as turn-taking 36–37
Duncan, S. 70

Edelsky, C. 37, 83
Edmundson, W. J. 18
engaged actor 30–32
Erickson, F. and J. Shultz 50, 115
Erting, C. 59
Ervin-Tripp, S. 23
ethnography of communication 19–21

Fasold, R. 10
Fenton, S. 32
Fowler, Y. 33
Frishberg, N. 104

Garfinkel, H. 18
Gentile, A. 40, 43
Gerver, D. 25
Goffman, E. 12, 17–18, 30, 44, 45,
    46, 63, 80, 104, 108, 111, 112,
    120, 121
Gumperz, J. 11, 12, 13–14, 17, 23, 50,
    80, 112

Harris, Z. 3
Hatim, B. and I. Mason 27–28, 35
Hymes, D. 20, 23, 40–41, 47

Ingram, R. 26
interactional sociolinguistics 12–18
Interpreter, the 61–63
interpreter/translator
    as ethnographers 126
    as negotiator 6, 27
    decision-making process 84–94
    interpreter role 7, 30, 60, 62–65,
        104–105, 106–111, 115–121,
        123–124
    neutrality 105, 124
    responsibilities and obligations
        64–66, 123
    talking to an interpreter 106–111,
        112–114
interpreting
    as a cognitive process 21–22
    as a communicative process 27,
        127–128
    as a conversational activity 45–46
    as a description 40–41
    as a discourse event
        44–46, 122–123
    as a speech event 24, 44–46
    as interaction 30–32
    as power 87–88
interpretive studies 51–52

James, D. and J. Drakich 83
Johnstone, B. 118

Kochman, T. 11, 21

Labov, W. 48
lag 74–84
    learning about lag 80–85
    lengthy lag 77–80
    regular lag 76–77
Lakoff, G. and M. Johnson 102
Lambert, S. 25
Lane, H. 59
Larson, M. 117
listening behaviors 57

managing communication 99–100
    managing flow of talk 3–4,
        32–34, 93, 109–110
    managing simultaneous talk 83–93
    managing turns 4, 67–68, 73–74
McDermott, R. and H. Tylbor 46, 72
Metzger, M. 33–35, 40, 44, 75, 96,
    104, 107, 110, 111, 124
Moser-Mercer, B. 25, 102
Murray, S. 37, 83

natural silence 74–75
Nida, E. 23, 117

O'Connell, D.C., S. Kowal, and
    E. Kaltenbacher 38
overlapping speech
    as interruption 83
overlapping speech/talk 37–38,
    83–84

participant alignment 111–114,
    119–121
participant pauses 75–76

participant roles 63–66
participation framework 112–114
Phillips, S. 11
playback interviews 50–51
Potter, J. and M. Wetherell 9
production formats 112
Professor, the 56–58

questions
  about interpreting 12, 43, 92, 96,
    107, 127
  for research 126–127

reception formats 112
Reddy, M. 102, 127, 128
Reichman, R. 9
Roberts, R. 40, 43
role expectations 104–105
role performance 18, 101–121,
    123–124
Roy, C. 40, 44, 45

Sacks, H., E. Schegloff, and G. Jefferson 18, 19, 36–37, 50, 68, 76
Schiffrin, D. 9, 10, 11, 13, 14, 20, 22,
    41, 48, 80, 111
Scollon, R. and S. Scollon 21
Seleskovitch, D. 26
Shuy, R. 25
social organization 17–18
SPEAKING 20–21
speech act 20, 41

speech community 41–42
speech event 20, 41
speech situation 20, 41
Stubbs, M. 10
Student, the 58–61

Tannen, D. 12, 16–17, 21, 37, 38, 45,
    48, 50, 51, 73, 80, 83, 111, 118
teaching interpreting 125–126
translation 23–25
turn-taking 4, 36–39, 67–100
  creating turns 4, 73–74
  decisions about turns 92–93
  ignoring a turn 89–91
  interpreter turns 93–98
  offering a turn 93–95
  overlapping turns 83–93
  regular turns 68–72
  speaker turns 5
  stopping a turn 85–89
  taking a turn 96–99
  turns with lag 74–83

utterances 10

Van Dijk, T. 9, 10
videotaping interaction 48–49

Wadensjö, C. 18, 22, 30–32, 33, 40,
    44, 104, 111, 112, 113, 120, 121,
    123, 124, 126
Winston, E. 118

Lightning Source UK Ltd.
Milton Keynes UK
27 June 2010

156142UK00004B/18/A